Data Wrangling with R

Hands on Practice for Beginners

Data Analytics Curriculum, LLC

About the Publisher

Data Analytics Curriculum

Data Analytics Curriculum, LLC creates approachable, visually engaging educational materials that make data science and technology accessible for learners from high school to college and independent study.

Please see our website or TPT online store for additional titles and resources such as slides, additional book forms, content (non lab) textbooks to accompany these labs, solution guides and other resources to help you teach and learn.

Additional resources available:

Website: https://www.dataanalyticscurriculum.com

Contents

Contents

Lab 1

Intro to R and RStudio

What is R and Why Use It?

R is a powerful and free programming language created specifically for statistical computing and data analysis. It has become popular across various fields such as data analytics, machine learning, and statistical analysis due to its extensive range of specialized packages tailored for data manipulation and interpretation. One of R's key strengths lies in its excellent data visualization capabilities, which allow users to create clear and insightful graphics. Additionally, it boasts strong libraries that support both statistical methods and machine learning techniques, making it a versatile tool for data professionals.

The language also benefits from a large and active community that contributes to its continuous improvement and offers support to users. Complementing R is RStudio, an Integrated Development Environment (IDE) that enhances the user experience by providing a more accessible interface, features like syntax highlighting, and various tools that help streamline the management of data projects, making it easier for both beginners and experienced users to work efficiently with R.

Part 1: Installing R and RStudio

Step 1: Download and Install R

Visit the R Project website: Go to https://www.r-project.org/

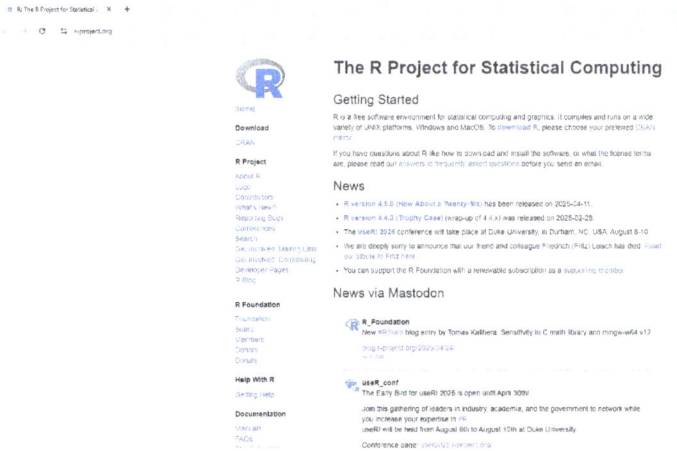

To install R, start by clicking on "CRAN" (Comprehensive R Archive Network) in the left sidebar of the website. Next, choose a mirror location that is close to you—any mirror in the USA works well for users in the United States. Then, select your operating system. For Windows, click on "Download R for Windows," then "base," and finally "Download R 4.x.x for Windows." Mac users should click on "Download R for macOS" and download the appropriate .pkg file for their system. If you are using Linux, follow the specific instructions provided for your distribution. Once the download is complete, run the installer and proceed with the default settings by clicking "Next" through the installation prompts.

Step 2: Download and Install RStudio

Note: You must install R first before installing RStudio, as RStudio requires R to function.

Visit RStudio's website: Go to https://posit.co/downloads/

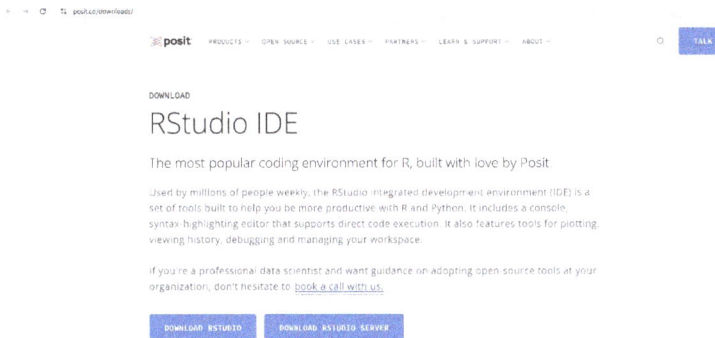

To install RStudio, scroll down the webpage until you find the section for RStudio Desktop, which is the free version. Click on "Download RStudio Desktop," then choose and download the installer that matches your operating system. Once the download is complete, run the installer and proceed with the default settings by simply clicking "Next" through the setup process.

Step 3: Verify Installation

Open RStudio (not R directly - we'll always use RStudio)

You should see a window with four panes (or three if it's your first time). In the bottom-left pane (Console), you should see something like:

If you see this, congratulations! You're ready to start using R.

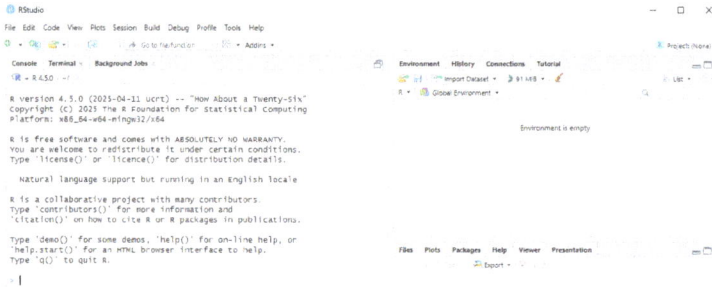

Part 2: The RStudio Interface

When you open RStudio, you'll see several panes. Initially there are three however go under file and do new R Script and the Script Editor appears.

Script Editor (Top-Left)

The Script Editor, located in the top-left panel of RStudio, is where you write and save your R scripts. It functions like a text editor specifically designed for writing R code, allowing you to organize and save your work for future use. From this panel, you can easily run individual lines or entire sections of code directly to the Console, making it a convenient space for developing and testing your code as you work through data analysis tasks.

4

Console (Bottom-Left)

The Console, found in the bottom-left panel of RStudio, is where R commands are executed. You can type commands directly into this space and see the results appear immediately below, making it useful for quick tests or interactive work. It's also where any code you run from the Script Editor will be processed, allowing you to view outputs, error messages, and other feedback in real time.

Environment/History (Top-Right)

The Environment/History panel, located in the top-right corner of RStudio, provides useful information about your current R session. The Environment tab displays all the data objects you've created, such as datasets, variables, and functions, allowing you to keep track of what's available in your workspace. The History tab keeps a record of all the commands you've run, making it easy to review, reuse, or modify previous code without having to retype it from memory.

Files/Plots/Packages/Help (Bottom-Right)

The Files/Plots/Packages/Help panel, located in the bottom-right corner of RStudio, serves several important functions. The Files tab lets you browse the files and folders on your computer, making it easy to locate and open your work. The Plots tab displays any graphs or visualizations you generate in R, allowing you to review and navigate through them. The Packages tab is where you can manage your R packages—these are add-on tools that extend R's capabilities, and you can install, load, or update them from this tab. Finally, the Help tab provides access to R's built-in documentation, offering detailed explanations and usage examples for functions and packages whenever you need guidance.

Part 3: Basic R Concepts

As a data analytics student, you'll primarily be running existing scripts rather than writing code from scratch. THIS IS NOT A PROGRAMMING COURSE OR BOOK. It is nice to have a programming background however the focus here is on USING and modifying existing scripts to perform data analytics tasks. You should be able to do this with a minimal programming background and should need to do little programming from scratch.

Working with Scripts

To open an existing R script in RStudio, go to the File menu, click on "Open File," and then select your .R file from your computer. Once your script is open, you can run your code in several ways. To execute a single line, place your cursor on that line and press Ctrl+Enter on Windows or Cmd+Enter on Mac. If you want to run multiple lines at once, highlight the lines you want to run and use the same keyboard shortcut. To run the entire script all at once, press Ctrl+Shift+Enter on Windows or Cmd+Shift+Enter on Mac. These shortcuts make it easy to test and execute your code efficiently.

Watch the output of running the script in the Console.

Understanding R Objects

In R, an object is simply a named piece of data that you create and store in your workspace. If you're new to programming, think of an object as a container that holds something—like a number, a list of names, a dataset, or even a graph. When you run code in R, you're often creating or modifying these objects. For example, if you type x <- 5, you're creating an object named x that stores the number 5. R has different types of objects depending on what kind of data you're working with. These include vectors (lists of values), data frames (tables of data), matrices (grids of numbers), and more. Understanding objects is important because everything you do in R—whether analyzing data, creating plots, or running models—usually involves creating and using these objects.

When you run scripts, you'll create different types of data objects. Primarily we will be creating or reading data frame objects either by typing in data or uploading a csv file for use in this book.

R Code

```
# Numbers

my_number <- 5

# Text (character strings)

my_text <- "Hello Data Mining"

# Vectors (lists of values)

my_numbers <- c(1, 2, 3, 4, 5)

my_names <- c("Alice", "Bob", "Charlie")

# Data frames (like Excel spreadsheets)

my_data <- data.frame(

name = c("Alice", "Bob", "Charlie"),

age = c(25, 30, 35),

score = c(85, 92, 78)
```

```
)
```

Reading Data Files

Most data analytics work starts with loading data in a preexisting file. These files can be read into R – the most easy way is to use csv files as these have no meta data or formatting (they are clean). Other files such as Excel require special packages to be loaded (see below on definition of a package). After data is loaded several functions allow you to view the data easily to validate the upload before using the data in analytics.

R Code
```
# Reading CSV files

data <- read.csv("mydata.csv")

# Reading Excel files (requires readxl package)

library(readxl)

data <- read_excel("mydata.xlsx")

# Viewing your data

View(data) # Opens data in a new tab

head(data) # Shows first 6 rows

summary(data) # Shows basic statistics
```

Part 4: R Packages

R packages are collections of functions, data, and documentation that extend the basic functionality of R, making it easier to perform specialized types of analysis. You can think of them as add-on toolkits designed for specific tasks, such as data visualization, machine learning, time series analysis, or text mining. Most R packages are open source and are created and shared by members of the global R community, including researchers, developers, and data professionals. These packages are typically hosted on CRAN (the Comprehensive R Archive Network), which is the official repository, but others may also be found on platforms like GitHub. Installing a package is simple: you can use the install.packages("package_name") command in the Console, or you can go to the Packages tab in RStudio and use the interface to search for and install packages. Once installed, packages need to be loaded into your session using the library(package_name) function before you can use their tools.

Installing Packages

You only need to install a package once (downloading it form online source) and then it will live on your local machine (unless you delete the files where it is stored or otherwise alter things).

```
R Code
# Install a single packageinstall.packages("ggplot2")


# Install multiple packagesinstall.packages(c("dplyr", "tidyr",
"caret"))
```

Loading Packages

You need to load packages every time you start RStudio so that they are available in the current working project environment.

```
R Code
# Load a packagelibrary(ggplot2)

# Or multiple packages

library(dplyr)

library(tidyr)

library(caret)
```

Essential Packages for data analytics

Here are some packages often used in data analytics (some of which we will use in labs in coming chapters).

- **dplyr**: Data manipulation (filtering, sorting, summarizing)

- **ggplot2**: Creating beautiful visualizations

- **caret**: Machine learning and classification

- **randomForest**: Random forest algorithms

- **e1071**: Support vector machines and other ML algorithms

- **cluster**: Clustering analysis

- **arules**: Association rule mining

- **rpart**: Decision trees

Part 5: Common Script Patterns

When working with R scripts, you typically start by loading your dataset—for example, from a CSV file—and then perform a quick exploration to understand its size, column names, structure, and summary statistics. In R, many operations you perform are done using functions, which are like little machines or tools that take some input, process it, and give you an output. For example, read.csv() is a function that reads data from a CSV file and loads it into R. Functions always have a name followed by parentheses, where you put any information they need, called arguments. Here's how you might load data and explore it:

```
# Load data

data <- read.csv("sales_data.csv")

# Quick exploration

dim(data) # Dimensions (rows, columns)

names(data) # Column names

str(data) # Structure of data

summary(data) # Summary statistics
```

When working with data frames (tables), you can use the $ operator to access specific columns by name. For example, data$price refers to the "price" column inside the dataset, letting you analyze or plot that specific variable.

In R, functions are individual commands or tools that perform specific tasks, such as calculating a mean or creating a plot. On the other hand, packages are collections of related functions and datasets bundled together to extend R's capabilities. Think of packages as toolkits or libraries that you install and load when you want extra features beyond base R. For example, the ggplot2 package contains many functions specifically designed for advanced data visualization.

After loading and exploring data, you often use functions to create simple visualizations or calculate basic statistics. For example, plot() creates a scatterplot, hist() creates a histogram, and mean() calculates the average value of a variable. Here are some examples:

R Code

```
# Create simple plots


# Scatter plot of price vs. quantity
plot(data$price, data$quantity)


hist(data$price) # Histogram of price


# Basic statistics


mean(data$price) # Mean price


median(data$price) # Median price


table(data$category) # Frequency count of categories
```

Part 6: Tips for Success

Set Your Working Directory

In R, the working directory is the folder on your computer where R looks for files to read and where it saves files by default. It's important to set your working directory to the location where your data files are stored so that you can easily load and save files without typing long file paths. You can set the working directory in R using the setwd() function with the path to your folder, for example:

```
R Code
setwd("C:/Users/YourName/Documents/DataMining").
```

Alternatively, if you're using RStudio, you can set it through the menu by going to the menu bar and Session → Set Working Directory → Choose Directory and selecting the appropriate folder. Setting your working directory correctly helps keep your projects organized and makes working with data files smoother.

File Management

When working in R, it's important to regularly save your progress to avoid losing any of your code or data. The scripts you write in R, which contain your R code, can be saved by pressing Ctrl+S on Windows or Cmd+S on a Mac. These script files usually have the extension .R. Saving your script means your code is safely stored on your computer and can be opened, edited, or run again later without starting from scratch.

Beyond saving scripts, R has something called a workspace, which you can think of as the current memory of your R session. The workspace holds all the data objects, variables, and functions you have created during your work.

Saving the workspace means saving everything you've done so far so that when you come back later, you don't have to reload or recreate all your data and settings — you can pick up exactly where you left off.

To keep everything related to a specific analysis or project organized, RStudio offers a helpful feature called Projects. A project bundles together all your scripts, data files, workspace, and any other documents into a single folder. This way, when you open a project, all the files and information you need for that particular task are in one place. This organization is especially useful if you are working on multiple assignments or analyses at the same time because it prevents files from getting mixed up or lost.

You can create a new project easily in RStudio by going to File → New Project. Using projects helps make your workflow smoother and your work more manageable. So, in summary, regularly save your .R scripts to keep your code safe, save your workspace to keep your data and variables intact, and use RStudio projects to keep everything related to your work well-organized.

Getting Help

When you're working in R, it's common to need help understanding what a function does or how to use it. A strength of R is the well written internal help support system. One way to get help is by typing commands directly in the Console. For example, if you want to learn about the mean() function, you can type ?mean and press Enter, and R will show the documentation for that function. Similarly, if you want to search for help on a topic or keyword, like "clustering," you can type ??clustering to find all related help pages.

In addition to these commands, RStudio provides a very useful Help pane located in the bottom-right corner of the interface. This Help pane allows you to search for functions, packages, and topics without needing to remember the exact commands. You can simply type a keyword or function name into the search box, and relevant help files and guides will appear for you

to browse. Clicking on any of these entries will open detailed documentation, including examples of how to use the function, explanations of its
arguments, and additional resources.

Using both the help commands (? and ??) in the Console and the Help pane
in RStudio gives you quick and easy access to the information you need,
making it much easier to learn and troubleshoot as you work with R.

Common Errors and Solutions

As you run script in R the Console will have error messages. Get familiar with
what these mean in case you need to trouble shoot.

Error: "Object not found"

- Solution: Make sure you've run the code that creates the object

- Check spelling and capitalization (R is case-sensitive)

Error: "Package not found"

- Solution: Install the package first with install.packages("packagename")

Error: "Cannot find file"

- Solution: Check your working directory and file path

- Use getwd() to see current directory

Best Practices for Script Users

When working with scripts, start by reading the comments—these are lines
beginning with # that often explain what each part of the code does. Avoid
running the entire script all at once right away; instead, run it section by
section to better understand how it works and catch errors early. As you
go, check the Environment pane to confirm that variables and objects are

being created as expected. Keep your data files well-organized by placing them in the same folder as your scripts, which helps avoid file path issues. Finally, always make a backup copy of the original script before making any changes, so you can easily revert if needed.

Lab 2

Sorting Data in R

Sorting involves rearranging the rows according to the values in one or more columns. This step helps reveal patterns, identify potential errors, and improves the readability of tables. In R sorting can be performed using base R functions or using the popular tidyverse dplyr package, which offers intuitive and flexible data manipulation tools.

In this lab, you will learn how to sort datasets by single or multiple columns, apply both ascending and descending order sorting, and use both base R and dplyr approaches to accomplish this.

Lesson Steps

Step 1: Create a Sample Dataset

We'll begin by creating a small dataset with three columns: Name, Age, and Date.

R Code

```r
# Create a small data frame

data <- data.frame(
  Name = c("Alice", "Brian", "Carlos", "Dana"),
  Age = c(22, 30, 25, 28),
  Date = as.Date(c(
    "2023-01-05", "2022-12-20",
    "2023-01-10", "2023-01-01"
  ))
)

# View the original data

data
```

Output

```
##      Name Age       Date
## 1  Alice  22 2023-01-05
## 2  Brian  30 2022-12-20
## 3 Carlos  25 2023-01-10
## 4   Dana  28 2023-01-01
```

Step 2: Sorting with Base R

Sort by Age (Ascending)

Ascending order means sorting values from smallest to largest. For numbers, this means going from low to high (e.g., 1, 2, 3, 10). For text, it means sorting alphabetically from A to Z. In dates, it means arranging from the earliest to the latest. Ascending order is often the default when sorting data, as it helps organize information in a logical, easy-to-read way.

Use the order() function to sort the rows based on the `Age` column. This rearranges the rows from the youngest to the oldest.

R Code
```
# Sort by Age in ascending order

sorted_data <- data[order(data$Age), ]
sorted_data
```

Output
```
##       Name Age       Date
## 1   Alice  22 2023-01-05
## 3  Carlos  25 2023-01-10
## 4    Dana  28 2023-01-01
## 2   Brian  30 2022-12-20
```

Sort by Age (Descending)

To sort in descending order, use a minus sign – before the numeric column.

R Code
```
# Sort by Age in descending order

sorted_data <- data[order(-data$Age), ]
sorted_data
```

Output

```
##       Name Age        Date
## 2   Brian  30 2022-12-20
## 4    Dana  28 2023-01-01
## 3  Carlos  25 2023-01-10
## 1   Alice  22 2023-01-05
```

Sort by Date

You can sort dates the same way either descending or ascending order.

R Code

```r
# Sort by Date in ascending order

sorted_data <- data[order(data$Date), ]
sorted_data
```

Output

```
##       Name Age        Date
## 2   Brian  30 2022-12-20
## 4    Dana  28 2023-01-01
## 1   Alice  22 2023-01-05
## 3  Carlos  25 2023-01-10
```

Sort by Multiple Columns

To sort by more than one column, pass them into function order().

R Code
```
# Sort by Age, then Date


sorted_data <- data[order(data$Age, data$Date), ]
sorted_data
```

Output
```
##      Name Age        Date
## 1  Alice   22 2023-01-05
## 3 Carlos   25 2023-01-10
## 4   Dana   28 2023-01-01
## 2  Brian   30 2022-12-20
```

Step 3: Sorting with dplyr::arrange()

In R, you can sort data using built-in base R functions, but many users prefer the dplyr package for its simplicity and clarity. dplyr is part of the tidyverse collection of packages designed to make data manipulation tasks easier. It uses intuitive, verb-like functions that describe what you want to do with your data. For sorting, dplyr provides the arrange() function, which offers a cleaner and more readable way to sort rows by one or more columns.

Load the package

If you haven't already installed `dplyr`, do so first.

R Code
```
# Install if not already installed

options(repos = c(CRAN = "https://cran.r-project.org"))
install.packages("dplyr")   # Run only once
library(dplyr)
```

Sort by Age (Ascending)

This code sorts the dataset by the Age column in ascending order using the arrange() function from the dplyr package. Smaller ages will appear at the top, and larger ages at the bottom.

R Code
```
# Sort by Age using dplyr

sorted_data <- arrange(data, Age)
sorted_data
```

Output
```
##       Name Age        Date
## 1    Alice  22 2023-01-05
## 2   Carlos  25 2023-01-10
## 3     Dana  28 2023-01-01
## 4    Brian  30 2022-12-20
```

Sort by Age (Descending)

By default, arrange() sorts in ascending order. To sort in descending order, you wrap the column name with the desc() function inside arrange().

R Code
```
# Sort by Age descending using dplyr


sorted_data <- arrange(data, desc(Age))
sorted_data
```

Output
```
##       Name Age       Date
## 1   Brian  30 2022-12-20
## 2    Dana  28 2023-01-01
## 3  Carlos  25 2023-01-10
## 4   Alice  22 2023-01-05
```

Sort by Date

Use arrange() to sort the dataset by the Date column in ascending order, placing earlier dates first.

R Code
```
# Sort by Date ascending


sorted_data <- arrange(data, Date)
sorted_data
```

23

Output

```
##      Name Age       Date
## 1  Brian  30 2022-12-20
## 2   Dana  28 2023-01-01
## 3  Alice  22 2023-01-05
## 4 Carlos  25 2023-01-10
```

Sort by Multiple Columns

Sort by multiple columns means arranging the data by one column first, and then by another column to break ties. For example, you sort by Age first, and if two people have the same Age, then you sort those by Date. This helps organize data more precisely.

R Code

```
# Sort by Age, then Date

sorted_data <- arrange(data, Age, Date)
sorted_data
```

Output

```
##      Name Age       Date
## 1  Alice  22 2023-01-05
## 2 Carlos  25 2023-01-10
## 3   Dana  28 2023-01-01
## 4  Brian  30 2022-12-20
```

Wrap-Up

In this lab, you learned how to sort data using both base R and package dplyr. The order() function provides flexibility, while arrange() from dplyr offers clearer syntax for chaining with other data manipulation functions.

Exercises

Practice with Sorting Data

In this lab, you'll practice sorting datasets in R using both base R (order()) and the dplyr package (arrange()). You'll work with two small, custom datasets and apply ascending and descending sorts, including on multiple columns. Each question requires a short answer—either output from R, a one-sentence interpretation, or a sorted table.

Dataset 1: Exam Scores

This dataset shows test results for a group of students, including their names, scores, and the date they took the exam.

```
R Code
exam_data <- data.frame(
  Student = c(
    "Liam", "Emma", "Noah",
    "Olivia", "Mason"
  ),
  Score = c(88, 95, 79, 92, 85),
  ExamDate = as.Date(c(
    "2023-03-10", "2023-03-12",
    "2023-03-08", "2023-03-10",
    "2023-03-09"
  ))
)
```

1. Sort exam_data by Score in ascending order using base R. Paste the output.

2. Now sort by Score in descending order using dplyr::arrange(). Paste the output.

3. Sort the data by ExamDate, then Score (both ascending) using base R. What is the name of the student who took the test first and scored lowest on that date?

4. Sort by Student name in alphabetical order using dplyr. What is the last name listed?

5. Which students scored above 85 after March 9, 2023? First filter, then sort by Score descending. Paste the result and state how many students matched.

Dataset 2: Product Shipments

This dataset represents a small log of products shipped, with their weight, destination zone, and shipping date.

```
R Code
shipments <- data.frame(
  Product = c(
    "Tablet", "Monitor", "Keyboard",
    "Laptop", "Mouse"
  ),
  Weight = c(1.2, 5.5, 0.9, 2.4, 0.3),
  ShipDate = as.Date(c(
    "2023-05-12", "2023-05-10",
    "2023-05-14", "2023-05-13", "2023-05-11"
  ))
)
```

6. Sort shipments by Weight in ascending order using base R. Paste the

sorted table.

7. Using dplyr, sort the data by ShipDate in descending order. Which item was shipped most recently?

8. Sort by Weight descending, then ShipDate ascending using base R. Which product is first in the list?

9. Which products weigh more than 1.0 and were shipped before May 13? Sort by ShipDate ascending.

10. Create a new column called WeightCategory where anything under 1 kg is labeled "Light" and the rest "Heavy". Sort by this new column, then by ShipDate. Paste the sorted table.

Dataset 3: City Temperatures

This dataset contains average daily temperatures recorded in various cities.

```
R Code
weather <- data.frame(
  City = c(
    "Miami", "Denver", "Seattle",
    "Phoenix", "Boston"
  ),
  TempC = c(29.4, 21.1, 18.2, 33.5, 22.0),
  Date = as.Date(c(
    "2023-07-01", "2023-07-01", "2023-07-01",
    "2023-07-01", "2023-07-01"
  ))
)
```

11. Sort weather by TempC in ascending order using dplyr. Which city had the lowest temperature?

12. Sort by City alphabetically, then by TempC descending. What are the top 3 cities in the sorted result?

13. Add a new column TempF that converts Celsius to Fahrenheit (TempF = TempC * 9/5 + 32). Sort by TempF descending and paste the full table.

Lab 3

Filtering Data in R

Filtering means selecting only the rows in your data that meet specific conditions. For example, you might want to view only users over age 30 or sales from a particular region. Filtering allows you to focus on relevant data, remove noise or outliers, and prepare subsets of data for visualization or modeling. In this lab, you will learn how to filter data using base R functions such as subset() and bracket notation, as well as how to use the filter() function from the dplyr package.

Lesson Steps

Step 1: Create Sample Data

We'll use a small dataset to demonstrate filtering techniques.

R Code
```
# Create a sample data frame


data <- data.frame(
    Name = c("Alice", "Bob", "Carlos", "Dana"),
    Age = c(22, 30, 25, 28),
    Gender = c("Female", "Male", "Male", "Female"),
    Score = c(88, 76, 91, 85)
)


# View the dataset


data
```

Output
```
##       Name Age Gender Score
## 1   Alice  22 Female    88
## 2     Bob  30   Male    76
## 3  Carlos  25   Male    91
## 4    Dana  28 Female    85
```

Step 2: Filtering with Base R

Using subset()

The subset() function lets you filter rows by asking a simple true-or-false question about each row. This question is called a logical condition. For example, you might ask, "Is the person's age greater than 30?" For each row, if the answer is true, that row is kept; if the answer is false, it is removed.

Logical conditions help you choose exactly which rows you want to work with.

This returns rows for Bob and Dana, because their age is over 25.

```
R Code
# Filter for rows where Age > 25


filtered_data <- subset(data, Age > 25)
filtered_data
```

```
Output
##    Name Age Gender Score
## 2  Bob  30    Male    76
## 4 Dana  28 Female    85
```

Using Bracket Notation

Bracket notation means using square brackets [ ] to pick certain parts of your data. When filtering rows, you put a condition inside the brackets to tell R which rows to keep. For example, data[data$Age > 30,] means: "Give me all the rows where Age is greater than 30." The part before the comma selects rows, and the part after the comma (which is empty here) means "keep all columns." It's a flexible way to manually choose data based on conditions.

Both methods produce the same filtered result.

R Code
```
# Same condition using bracket notation


filtered_data <- data[data$Age > 25, ]
filtered_data
```

Output
```
##    Name Age Gender Score
## 2  Bob  30   Male    76
## 4 Dana  28 Female    85
```

Multiple conditions

You can combine multiple conditions using & (and) or | (or).

This code filters the dataset to keep only rows where both conditions are true: the person's Age is greater than 25 and their Gender is Female. The & symbol means "and," so only rows meeting both criteria are included in filtered_data. The result shows all females older than 25 from your original data.

R Code
```
# Filter: Age > 25 AND Gender is Female


filtered_data <- subset(data, Age > 25 & Gender == "Female")
filtered_data
```

```
Output
##    Name Age Gender Score
## 4 Dana  28 Female    85
```

Step 3: Filtering with dplyr

The dplyr package makes filtering data easier with a cleaner, more readable syntax. Instead of using complicated code, you can use the filter() function to select rows that meet your conditions in a straightforward way.

Load the package

If you haven't already installed dplyr, do so once:

```
R Code
# Install if not already installed

options(repos = c(CRAN = "https://cran.r-project.org"))
install.packages("dplyr")  # Run once
library(dplyr)
```

Use filter()

The filter() function from the dplyr package helps you select rows that meet specific conditions. For example, to keep only rows where the Score is greater than 80, you write:

35

R Code
```
# Filter rows where Score > 80


filtered_data <- filter(data, Score > 80)
filtered_data
```

Output
```
##      Name Age Gender Score
## 1  Alice  22 Female    88
## 2 Carlos  25   Male    91
## 3   Dana  28 Female    85
```

This returns all rows where the Score column is above 80.

You can also combine multiple conditions by separating them with commas. When you do this, all conditions must be true (like an "and").

This keeps only rows where the person is older than 25 and has a score above 80.

R Code
```
# Age > 25 AND Score > 80


filtered_data <- filter(
   data, Age > 25,
   Score > 80
)
filtered_data
```

Output
```
##    Name Age Gender Score
## 1 Dana  28 Female    85
```

To filter based on text or categories, use == to check for equality. For example, to select only males, write:

R Code
```
# Gender is Male

filtered_data <- filter(data, Gender == "Male")
filtered_data
```

Output
```
##      Name Age Gender Score
## 1    Bob  30   Male    76
## 2 Carlos  25   Male    91
```

This returns all rows where the Gender column exactly matches "Male."

Using filter() makes your code easier to read and write compared to base R methods, especially when working with multiple conditions.

Wrap-Up

In this lab, you practiced filtering rows using base R's subset() function and bracket notation, as well as the filter() function from the dplyr package, which offers a more readable syntax. Filtering is a foundational skill for transforming messy data into a clean, workable format. Whether you are narrowing down specific time periods, excluding missing values, or focusing on high performers, filtering allows you to work with only the information that is relevant to your analysis. Mastering filtering helps make your data analysis more precise and efficient.

Exercises

Filtering Data in R

In this lab, you will practice filtering data in R using both base R and the dplyr package. Filtering allows you to isolate rows that meet specific conditions, such as particular age ranges, score thresholds, or categories.

Dataset 1: Library Borrowing Records

This dataset shows information about books borrowed from a library, including the title, borrower's age, book type, and overdue status.

```
R Code
library_data <- data.frame(
  Title = c(
    "Solar Power", "Ancient Civilizations",
    "AI Today", "The Great Outdoors",
    "Intro to R"
  ),
  Age = c(34, 17, 22, 29, 19),
  Type = c(
    "Nonfiction", "Nonfiction",
    "Technology",
    "Travel", "Technology"
  ),
  Overdue = c(TRUE, FALSE, FALSE, TRUE, FALSE)
)
```

1. Use base R to filter for borrowers over age 25. Paste the resulting table.

2. Use dplyr::filter() to find books where Type == "Technology". Paste the

result.

3. Filter for rows where books are not overdue. What titles appear?

4. Filter for rows where `Age <= 20` and `Type == "Technology"` using base R. Paste the result.

5. How many overdue books were borrowed by users under age 30? Use `dplyr` and give the count.

Dataset 2: Gym Memberships

This dataset contains information about gym members and their fitness class attendance.

```
R Code
gym_data <- data.frame(
  Member = c(
    "Jordan", "Riley", "Chris",
    "Taylor", "Morgan"
  ),
  Age = c(27, 45, 32, 38, 23),
  Classes_Attended = c(12, 4, 8, 6, 15),
  Plan = c(
    "Basic", "Premium", "Premium",
    "Basic", "Basic"
  )
)
```

6. Use base R to filter members on the "Basic" plan. Who are they?

7. Use dplyr to filter for members who attended more than 10 classes. Paste the filtered table.

8. Find members over 30 who are on the "Premium" plan. Use base R.

9. Filter for members under 30 and with fewer than 10 classes. Use `dplyr` and paste results.

10. Add a column called `HighAttendance` where members with 10+ classes are marked "Yes" and others "No". Then filter for "Yes" and sort by Age.

Dataset 3: Daily Step Counts

This optional dataset shows daily step counts recorded on fitness devices for different users.

```
R Code
steps_data <- data.frame(
  User = c("Eva", "Noah", "Liam", "Mia", "Zoe"),
  Steps = c(10450, 8200, 9600, 12000, 7200),
  ActiveDay = c(TRUE, FALSE, TRUE, TRUE, FALSE)
)
```

11. Use `dplyr` to filter for users with more than 9500 steps. Who are they?

12. Filter for users who did not have an active day but still walked more than 7000 steps.

13. Create a new column GoalMet where Steps >= 10000 equals "Yes", otherwise "No". Filter to show only those who met the goal.

Lab 4

Conditional Formatting in R

Conditional formatting is a way to visually data based on specific rules. In spreadsheets like Excel, this often means changing a cell's color or font when certain conditions are met. In R, you can't format cells directly as it is not a spreadsheet environment. Instead, to do the equivalent of Excel's conditional formatting you flag, categorize, or annotate data using logical conditions.

This lab will show you how to flag numeric values that fall outside expected ranges, such as outliers, and how to identify missing or inconsistent values in text columns. You will also learn to apply conditional logic using functions like ifelse() and case_when().

Lesson Steps

Step 1: Create a Dataset with Numeric Values

Let's start with a simple dataset that shows daily water consumption (in liters) for 10 students.

R Code

```
# Install if not already installed

options(repos = c(CRAN = "https://cran.r-project.org"))
install.packages("dplyr")  # Run only once
library(dplyr)
```

R Code

```
# Example dataset: daily water consumption in liters

water_data <- tibble(
  Student_ID = 1:10,
  Water_Consumption = c(
    1.2, 0.4, 2.3, 5.6, 3.1, 0.3,
    4.8, 1.9, 6.2, 2.0
  )
)
print(water_data)
```

Output

```
## # A tibble: 10 x 2
##    Student_ID Water_Consumption
##         <int>             <dbl>
##  1           1               1.2
##  2           2               0.4
##  3           3               2.3
##  4           4               5.6
##  5           5               3.1
##  6           6               0.3
##  7           7               4.8
##  8           8               1.9
##  9           9               6.2
## 10          10               2
```

Step 2: Flag Outliers in Numeric Data

Suppose normal water consumption is between 0.5 and 5.0 liters per day. We can use ifelse() to create a new column that flags out-of-range values.

R Code

```
# Flag outliers

water_data$Flag <- with(water_data,
   ifelse(Water_Consumption < 0.5 | Water_Consumption > 5.0,
       "Outlier", "OK")
)

print(water_data)
```

Output

```
## # A tibble: 10 x 3
##    Student_ID Water_Consumption Flag
##         <int>             <dbl> <chr>
##  1          1               1.2 OK
##  2          2               0.4 Outlier
##  3          3               2.3 OK
##  4          4               5.6 Outlier
##  5          5               3.1 OK
##  6          6               0.3 Outlier
##  7          7               4.8 OK
##  8          8               1.9 OK
##  9          9               6.2 Outlier
## 10         10               2   OK
```

You now have a new Flag column that marks outliers. These flags can be used to investigate or filter the data later.

Step 3: Create a Dataset with Text Values

Now let's work with a dataset where the issue is missing or inconsistent text values, such as labels or categories.

```
R Code
# Dataset with a text column 'Category'


data <- tibble(
  ID = 1:6,
  Category = c("A", "B", NA, "", "Unknown", "A")
)
```

This dataset contains a mix of valid, missing, and inconsistent values in the Category column.

Step 4: Apply Conditional Formatting to Text Data

We will use the case_when() function from the dplyr package to label rows based on custom rules. If the Category value is NA or an empty string, it will be flagged as "Missing." If the Category is "Unknown," it will be flagged as "Inconsistent." Otherwise, the row will be labeled as "OK."

The | symbol means "or," so the first rule applies if either condition is true. This way, every row gets a clear label based on its category.

R Code
```
# Flag missing and inconsistent categories

data$Flag <- case_when(
    is.na(data$Category) | data$Category == "" ~ "Missing",
    data$Category == "Unknown" ~ "Inconsistent",
    TRUE ~ "OK"
)

print(data)
```

Output
```
## # A tibble: 6 x 3
##       ID Category   Flag
##    <int> <chr>      <chr>
## 1     1 "A"        OK
## 2     2 "B"        OK
## 3     3  <NA>      Missing
## 4     4 ""         Missing
## 5     5 "Unknown"  Inconsistent
## 6     6 "A"        OK
```

This results in a new Flag column that clearly identifies rows needing review or cleanup.

Wrap-Up

In this lab, you practiced simulating conditional formatting in R by creating new flag columns. You used the ifelse() function for simple numeric thresholds and the case_when() function for more complex or categorical conditions. This type of logic is important for data cleaning, quality checks, and identifying anomalies in your dataset. Although R does not change cell colors like Excel, adding flag columns with labels helps you organize, filter, and visualize data quality programmatically.

Exercises

Conditional Formatting in R

Conditional formatting helps you flag rows in your dataset based on rules, such as values that are out of range or text labels that are missing or inconsistent. In R, you use functions like ifelse() or case_when() to simulate this process by adding flag columns. In this lab, you will create your own flags using both numeric and text conditions. You will work with multiple small datasets to apply conditional logic and clean your data.

Dataset 1: Student Exam Scores

This dataset contains exam scores for students and flags those who failed, passed, or earned honors.

```
R Code
exam_data <- data.frame(
  Student = c(
    "Alex", "Bri", "Chen", "Dana",
    "Eli", "Fatima"
  ),
  Score = c(92, 58, 77, 83, 45, 100)
)
```

1. Use the ifelse() function to create a column called Result that assigns "Fail" for scores below 60, "Pass" for scores between 60 and 89, and "Honors" for scores 90 and above. Paste your code and show the resulting dataset.

2. How many students received a result of "Honors," and what are their names?

3. Create a version of the dataset sorted by `Score` in descending order using either base R or `dplyr`.

4. Filter the dataset to show only students who received a result of "Pass," excluding both "Fail" and "Honors." Paste the output.

5. What is the average score of students who received a result of "Fail"?

Dataset 2: Product Orders

This dataset contains sample product orders, including category and order status.

R Code

```
orders <- data.frame(
  OrderID = 101:107,
  Category = c("Electronics", "", "Clothing",
               "Unknown", "Food", NA, "Clothing"),
  Status = c("Delivered", "Pending", "Cancelled",
             "Delivered", "Returned", "Pending",
             "Delivered")
)
```

6. Use the case_when() function to flag the Category column by assigning "Missing" if the value is an empty string or `NA`, "Inconsistent" if the value is "Unknown", and "OK" otherwise. Add this as a new column called Category_Flag and show the result.

7. Use the table() function to count how many rows fall under each value in the Category_Flag column.

8. Create a version of the dataset that includes only rows where the category flag is "OK". Paste the filtered table.

9. How many orders have a status of "Pending" and a flagged category of "Missing"?

10. Using dplyr, create a summary that shows the number of "Delivered" orders for each category flag.

Dataset 3: Air Quality Readings

This dataset includes air quality readings and flags dangerous pollution levels.

```
R Code
air_quality <- data.frame(
  Sensor_ID = 201:207,
  PM2.5 = c(
    9.1, 35.4, 55.5, 12.0,
    85.0, 150.2, 8.0
  )
)
```

11. Add a column named Air_Quality_Flag that assigns "Good" if PM2.5 is less than 12, "Moderate" if PM2.5 is between 12 and 35.4, and "Unhealthy" if PM2.5 is greater than 35.4. Use the `case_when()` function to create this column and show the result.

12. Which sensor recorded the highest PM2.5 level, and what was the corresponding air quality category?

13. Create a bar chart (optional) that shows how many readings fall into each air quality category. You may use either `ggplot2` or base R plotting functions.

Lab 5

Summarizing Data

Summarizing data in an aggregated summary table groups your data and calculates totals, counts, or averages. While Excel has a built-in pivot table feature, in R you can create similar summaries using functions like aggregate() and table(). In data wrangling, summary tables of counts (frequency tables) are especially helpful for checking for misspellings or inconsistent labels and spotting unusual patterns in your data.

Lesson Steps

Step 1: Create a Sample Dataset with an Error

We'll create a small dataset of sales, including a misspelling in the Color column.

R Code

```
# Sample sales data with a misspelled color


sales_data <- data.frame(
  Region = c(
    "East", "West", "East", "West",
    "North", "East", "South"
  ),
  Color = c(
    "Red", "Blue", "Yellow", "Red",
    "Yelow", "Blue", "Yellow"
  ),
  Sales = c(100, 150, 200, 130, 180, 120, 170)
)


print(sales_data)
```

Output

```
##    Region  Color Sales
## 1    East    Red   100
## 2    West   Blue   150
## 3    East Yellow   200
## 4    West    Red   130
## 5   North  Yelow   180
## 6    East   Blue   120
## 7   South Yellow   170
```

Step 2: Summarize Total Sales by Color

We'll group the data by Color and calculate both total sales per color and number of rows per color

```
R Code
# Summarize total sales by color

sales_summary <- aggregate(Sales ~ Color,
  data = sales_data,
  FUN = function(x) {
    c(
      Total = sum(x),
      Count = length(x)
    )
  }
)

print(sales_summary)
```

```
Output
##     Color Sales.Total Sales.Count
## 1    Blue         270           2
## 2     Red         230           2
## 3 Yellow         370           2
## 4  Yelow         180           1
```

You'll see both "Yellow" and "Yelow" listed separately. This signals a problem.

Step 3: Fix the Misspelling

Correct the typo by replacing "Yelow" with "Yellow" in the Color column.

```
R Code
# Correct the typo

sales_data$Color[sales_data$Color == "Yelow"] <- "Yellow"

print(sales_data)
```

```
Output
##    Region  Color Sales
## 1    East     Red   100
## 2    West    Blue   150
## 3    East Yellow   200
## 4    West     Red   130
## 5   North Yellow   180
## 6    East    Blue   120
## 7   South Yellow   170
```

Step 4: Create the Summary Again

Now that the typo is fixed, summarize again to see the cleaned version.

R Code
```
# Recalculate summary after cleaning

sales_summary_clean <- aggregate(Sales ~ Color,
  data = sales_data,
  FUN = function(x) {
    c(
      Total = sum(x),
      Count = length(x)
    )
  }
)

print(sales_summary_clean)
```

Output
```
##      Color Sales.Total Sales.Count
## 1    Blue          270           2
## 2     Red          230           2
## 3 Yellow          550           3
```

Now "Yellow" appears only once, with the correct combined totals and count.

Step 5: Count by Region

You can also count how many sales entries appear in each Region using table().

R Code
```
# Count how many entries per region


region_counts <- table(sales_data$Region)


print(region_counts)
```

Output
```
##
##   East North South  West
##      3     1     1     2
```

The result will be a summary table that shows the count of sales entries for each region. This helps you quickly see how many records belong to each group, giving an overview of the distribution of data across different regions.

Wrap-Up

In this lab, you learned how to create summary tables using the aggregate() function to group and summarize data. You practiced identifying data quality issues such as typos, then fixed these errors to produce cleaner, more accurate summaries. You also used the table() function to quickly count the number of records in each group. Creating summaries is a useful diagnostic technique that helps reveal potential problems in your data before analysis.

Exercises

Summarizing Data

In this exercise, you'll practice creating pivot-style summaries. These summaries help you detect inconsistencies, compute totals and counts by group, and check your data before analysis. You'll work with small datasets to explore data wrangling situations like spelling mistakes, inconsistent labels, and numeric summaries by group.

Dataset 1: Student Grades by Course and Instructor

```
R Code
grades_data <- data.frame(
  Student = c(
    "Amy", "Ben", "Cara", "Dan", "Ella",
    "Frank", "Gina", "Hank"
  ),
  Course = c(
    "Math", "Math", "Science", "Science",
    "Math", "Science", "Math", "Science"
  ),
  Instructor = c(
    "Lee", "Lee", "Khan", "Khan", "Le",
    "Khan", "Lee", "Khan"
  ),
  Grade = c(87, 92, 78, 85, 90, 88, 95, 84)
)
```

1. Use aggregate() to calculate the average grade per instructor. What do you observe about the instructor names?

2. Count how many students each instructor taught using table().

3. Combine "Lee" and "Le" into a single correct label, assuming the correct spelling is "Lee". Show the updated dataset.

4. Recalculate the average grade per instructor using aggregate() after fixing the spelling issue.

5. Create a summary that shows the average grade per Course and count how many students are enrolled in each course using table().

Dataset 2: Orders by Product and Region

```
R Code
orders <- data.frame(
  Product = c(
    "Pen", "Pencil", "Pen", "Marker",
    "Pen", "Pencil", "Marker", "Pencil"
  ),
  Region = c(
    "North", "South", "East", "West",
    "North", "South", "West", "East"
  ),
  Quantity = c(10, 15, 12, 20, 11, 14, 18, 17)
)
```

6. Use aggregate() to calculate the total quantity ordered for each product.

7. Calculate the number of orders per region using table().

8. Create a pivot-style summary showing the average quantity ordered per product.

9. Suppose the "Pencil" orders from the East region were misclassified and should be labeled "North." Update the dataset accordingly and show the result.

10. After the correction, calculate the total quantity ordered by Region again.

Lab 6

Functions for Data Cleaning

In R, functions are reusable blocks of code that perform specific tasks, making your work more efficient and consistent. There are two main types of functions you'll encounter. First, built-in functions like mean() or sum() are preloaded in R or included in packages. These are used for common tasks such as calculating averages or totals. Second, user-defined functions are ones you create yourself, usually to automate repetitive tasks or apply custom logic.

Functions are essential for cleaning, summarizing, and analyzing data, especially when working with large or messy datasets. In this lab, you'll explore how to use both types of functions for common data wrangling tasks.

Lesson Steps

Step 1: Clean and Standardize Text

Text data is often messy and inconsistent. We use string functions in R to standardize case, remove extra spaces, and combine words. The toupper() function changes all letters to uppercase, tolower() makes everything lowercase, and trimws() removes unwanted spaces at the beginning or end of a string. To join words into a single phrase, we use paste().

R Code
```
# Convert text to upper or lower case

toupper("excel")
```

Output
```
## [1] "EXCEL"
```

R Code
```
tolower("R IS POWERFUL")
```

Output
```
## [1] "r is powerful"
```

R Code
```
# Remove leading and trailing whitespace

trimws("  hello world  ")
```

Output
```
## [1] "hello world"
```

R Code
```
# Combine words into one phrase

paste("data", "cleaning", sep = " ")
```

Output
```
## [1] "data cleaning"
```

Step 2: Assign Labels Based on Conditions

We use the ifelse() function to label or categorize data based on conditions. This is helpful when transforming numeric data into categories like "High" or "Low". The function checks a condition and assigns one value if it's true and another if it's false. You can apply it to a single number or a whole vector.

R Code
```
# Label a single score

score <- 87
ifelse(score > 80, "High", "Low")
```

Output
```
## [1] "High"
```

R Code
```
# Label a vector of scores

scores <- c(50, 82, 91, 67)
ifelse(scores > 80, "High", "Low")
```

Output
```
## [1] "Low"  "High" "High" "Low"
```

Step 3: Work with Dates and Extract Components

Dates are important in analysis, and R provides tools to extract useful parts like year or month. Sys.Date() returns today's date. You can use as.Date() to turn a string into a date object. Once you have a date object, use format() to pull out the year ("%Y") or full month name ("%B").

R Code
```
# Get today's date

Sys.Date()
```

Output
```
## [1] "2025-07-29"
```

R Code
```
# Extract year and month

date <- as.Date("2025-06-03")
format(date, "%Y")
```

Output
```
## [1] "2025"
```

R Code
```
format(date, "%B")
```

Output
```
## [1] "June"
```

Step 4: Summarize Numeric Data with Statistics

You can summarize numeric data using basic statistical functions. The mean() function returns the average, median() finds the middle value, sd() calculates standard deviation (a measure of spread), and range() shows the minimum and maximum values.

R Code
```
# Numeric summary

numbers <- c(10, 20, 30, 40, 50)

mean(numbers)
```

Output
```
## [1] 30
```

R Code
```
median(numbers)
```

Output

```
## [1] 30
```

R Code

```
sd(numbers)
```

Output

```
## [1] 15.81139
```

R Code

```
range(numbers)
```

Output

```
## [1] 10 50
```

Step 5: Identify and Remove Missing Values

Missing values can cause errors or distort analysis. Use is.na() to check which values are missing (NA). To remove missing values from your data, use na.omit().

R Code
```
# Detect and remove NAs


data <- c(1, 2, NA, 4)


is.na(data)
```

Output
```
## [1] FALSE FALSE  TRUE FALSE
```

R Code
```
cleaned <- na.omit(data)
cleaned
```

Output
```
## [1] 1 2 4
## attr(,"na.action")
## [1] 3
## attr(,"class")
## [1] "omit"
```

Step 6: Write a Simple Custom Function

Writing your own function lets you reuse logic easily. In R, you define a function using function(). This example creates a function that adds two numbers and returns the result.

R Code
```
# Create and use a simple function

add_numbers <- function(a, b) {
  result <- a + b
  return(result)
}

add_numbers(5, 7)
```

Output
```
## [1] 12
```

Wrap-Up

You've now practiced using basic R functions that are essential building blocks for data cleaning. These included transforming text using case conversion and trimming, applying conditional logic with ifelse(), extracting parts of a date with format(), and computing simple statistics like the mean and standard deviation. You also learned how to identify and omit missing values, and how to write your own custom function using function().

Exercises

Functions for Data Cleaning

In this exercise, you will work with built-in and custom R functions to clean, transform, and analyze data.

Dataset 1: Employee Feedback Survey

This dataset contains employee names, ratings, and feedback collected via an online form. Some entries are messy or incomplete.

```
R Code
# Dataset 1: Employee feedback

employee_data <- data.frame(
  Name = c(
    " alice ", "BOB", "Clare", "daniel",
    "eve", NA
  ),
  Rating = c(4, 5, 3, 2, NA, 4),
  Feedback = c(
    "Great job", "EXCELLENT", "", "good",
    NA, "excellent"
  )
)
```

1. Clean the Name column by removing leading/trailing spaces and converting all names to title case (e.g., "Alice"). Show the result.

2. Identify which values in the Feedback column are missing or blank (""). Use a function to display TRUE for those values.

3. Replace all uppercase Feedback values with lowercase versions. Show the new version of the column.

4. Use ifelse() to create a new column Rating_Category where ratings ≥ 4 are "Positive", 3 is "Neutral", and below 3 is "Negative". Show the full dataset.

5. Remove rows where Rating or Feedback is missing (NA) using na.omit() and show the cleaned dataset.

Dataset 2: Shipment Logs

This dataset tracks delivery status and dates for shipped items. Some delivery dates are missing or improperly formatted.

```
R Code
# Dataset 2: Shipment logs

shipments <- data.frame(
  Package_ID = 101:106,
  Delivery_Date = c(
    "2025-05-10", "2025-05-12", NA,
    "2025-05-11", "invalid", "2025-05-13"
  ),
  Status = c(
    "Delivered", "Delivered", "Pending",
    "Delivered", "Pending", ""
  )
)
```

6. Use is.na() to check which delivery dates are missing (NA) and which ones are invalid ("invalid" is not an NA). Explain the difference in results.

7. Replace "invalid" with an actual date ("2025-05-14") in the Delivery_Date column and print the fixed dataset.

8. Convert all delivery dates to Date format using as.Date() and use format() to extract the weekday name (e.g., Monday, Tuesday).

9. Create a new column Status_Flag using ifelse() where "Delivered" becomes "Complete", and anything else becomes "Incomplete". Show the dataset.

10. Count how many shipments were delivered on a Monday. Use your weekday column and a summary function.

Dataset 3: Customer Purchases

This dataset includes information about product purchases. You'll calculate summary statistics and handle missing values.

```
R Code
# Dataset 3: Customer purchases

purchases <- data.frame(
  Customer_ID = 201:208,
  Product = c(
    "Tablet", "Phone", NA,
    "Laptop", "Tablet",
    "Laptop", "Phone", "Phone"
  ),
  Amount = c(
    300, 500, 450, 800, NA, 750,
    600, 500
  )
)
```

11. Use is.na() to identify missing values in the Product and Amount columns.

12. Use mean() and median() to summarize the Amount column.   Use na.omit() to exclude missing values.

13. Write a custom function named add_tax() that adds 8% tax to an amount and apply it to the Amount column (excluding NAs).

Lab 7

Graphical Analytics

Data visualizations are useful tools for detecting problems that might not be obvious from looking at tables or summary statistics. Charts can help you identify missing values, inconsistencies, outliers, or unusual patterns that could indicate issues with the data. While graphs don't replace formal statistical checks, they offer a quick and intuitive way to explore data quality.

In this lab, you'll work with a simulated dataset and use line charts, scatterplots, histograms, and boxplots to uncover potential problems. The dataset includes a few intentional errors—such as missing values, typos, and unrealistic sales figures—so you can practice identifying them and begin thinking about how to address them.

Lesson Steps

Step 1: Load and Preview the Data

The dataset includes daily drink sales along with temperature and drink type. Some values are intentionally flawed to simulate real-world messiness.

R Code

```
set.seed(123)

cafe_sales <- data.frame(
  Day = seq.Date(
    from = as.Date("2024-09-01"),
    by = "day", length.out = 60
  ),
  Temp = round(rnorm(60, mean = 68, sd = 10), 1),
  Drink = sample(c(
    "Latte", "Cold Brew", "Espresso",
    "Tea"
  ), 60, replace = TRUE),
  Sold = sample(20:150, 60, replace = TRUE)
)

cafe_sales$Weekday <- weekdays(cafe_sales$Day)

# Introduce errors

cafe_sales$Temp[c(5, 15)] <- NA
cafe_sales$Drink[c(8, 22)] <- "cold brew"
cafe_sales$Drink[30] <- "Espressso"
cafe_sales$Sold[12] <- 300
cafe_sales$Sold[27] <- -5
cafe_sales$Weekday[40] <- "saturdaay"
cafe_sales$Sold[45] <- NA

head(cafe_sales, 10)
```

Output

```
##             Day Temp      Drink Sold    Weekday
## 1   2024-09-01 62.4      Latte  102     Sunday
## 2   2024-09-02 65.7        Tea   58     Monday
## 3   2024-09-03 83.6   Espresso   73    Tuesday
## 4   2024-09-04 68.7   Espresso   67  Wednesday
## 5   2024-09-05   NA   Espresso   96   Thursday
## 6   2024-09-06 85.2 Cold Brew   102     Friday
## 7   2024-09-07 72.6 Cold Brew   130   Saturday
## 8   2024-09-08 55.3 cold brew    58     Sunday
## 9   2024-09-09 61.1      Latte   20     Monday
## 10  2024-09-10 63.5      Latte   49    Tuesday
```

Step 2: Create a Line Chart to View Trends Over Time

A line chart is useful for examining how drink sales change over time. By plotting each day's sales, we can observe patterns and spot any irregular points.

R Code

```
# Install if not already installed

options(repos = c(CRAN = "https://cran.r-project.org"))
install.packages('ggplot2')
library(ggplot2)
```

R Code
```
# Line chart of drink sales over time


ggplot(cafe_sales, aes(x = Day, y = Sold)) +
  geom_line(color = "#3D5A80") +
  geom_point() +
  labs(title = "Drinks Sold Over Time")
```

Drinks Sold Over Time

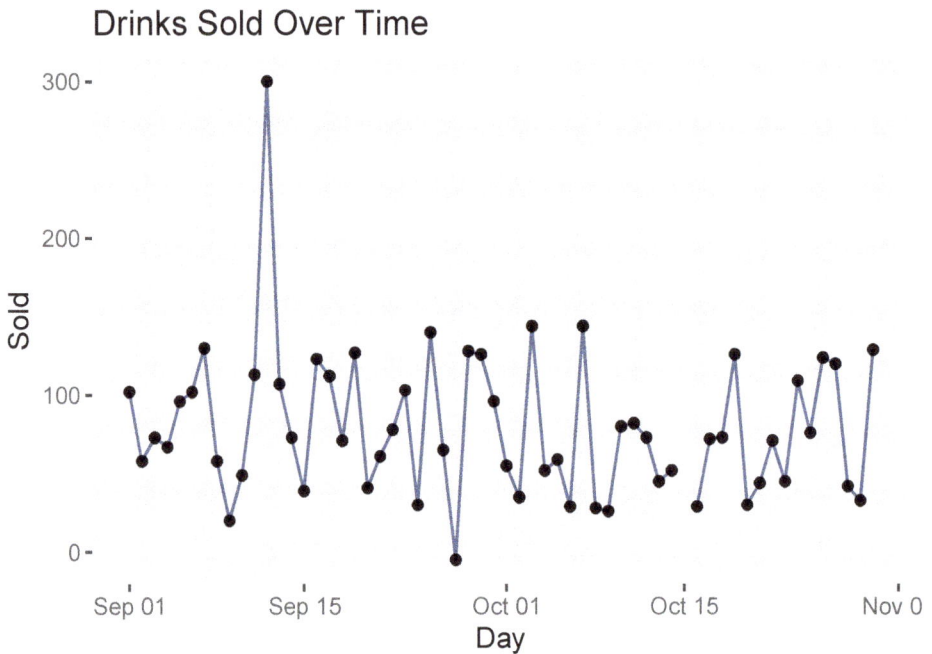

This chart shows how many drinks were sold each day. If you see sharp spikes or dips between adjacent days, that may indicate an error in recording the number sold. Also, any gaps where points are missing could suggest incomplete data for certain days.

Step 3: Use a Scatterplot to Examine the Relationship Between Temperature and Sales

A scatterplot allows us to see if there's a relationship between temperature and drink sales. Each point shows the temperature on a given day and how many drinks were sold.

R Code

```
# Scatterplot of temperature vs. sales
# colored by drink type

ggplot(cafe_sales, aes(x = Temp, y = Sold)) +
  geom_point(aes(color = Drink)) +
  labs(title = "Temperature vs. Drink Sales")
```

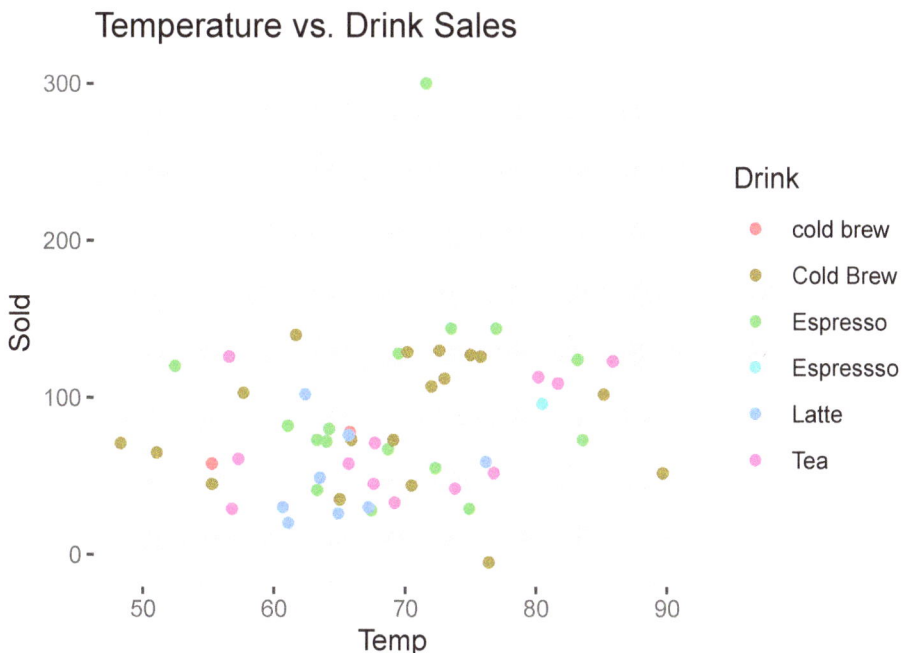

Temperature vs. Drink Sales

This chart helps you determine whether higher temperatures lead to more drink sales. You can also check if any points seem far outside the general pattern, which might reflect unrealistic values. Coloring by drink type can reveal if certain types behave differently, and unexpected colors may hint at typos in the drink names.

Step 4: Create a Histogram to See the Distribution of Sales

Histograms group numeric values into bins to show how often different ranges occur. This is helpful to understand the overall distribution of drink sales.

```
R Code
# Histogram of drink sales
ggplot(cafe_sales, aes(x = Sold)) +
  geom_histogram(binwidth = 10, fill = "#EE6C4D",
                 color = "black") +
  labs(title = "Distribution of Drink Sales",
       x = "Number of Drinks Sold", y = "Frequency")
```

Distribution of Drink Sales

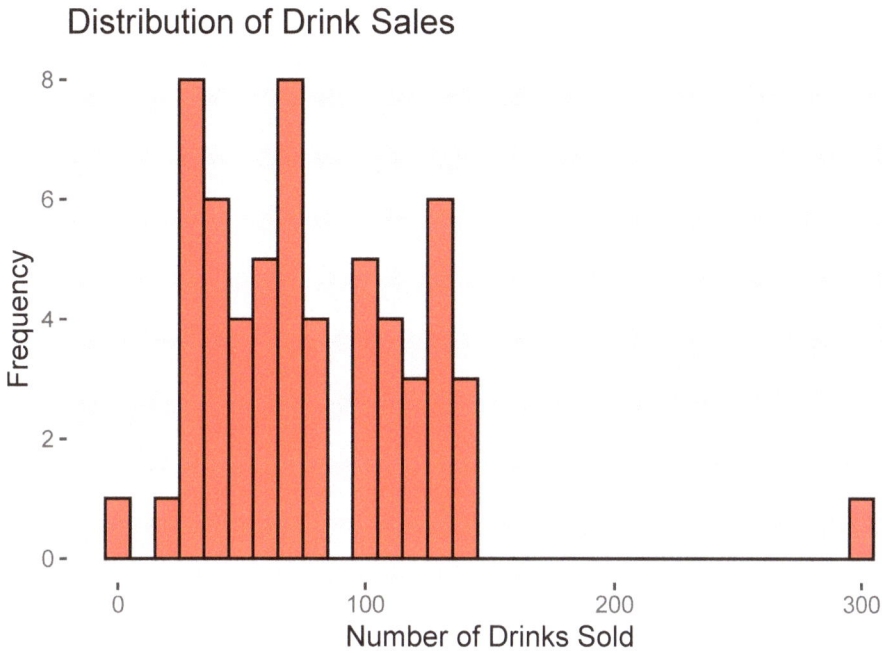

This histogram shows how common different sales amounts are. You can use this to check whether there are any sales values that happen much more or less often than others. If there are bars near zero or extremely high values that don't align with the rest, these might indicate possible data entry errors.

Step 5: Use a Boxplot to Compare Sales by Drink Type

Boxplots summarize distributions across categories and highlight possible outliers. This plot shows sales distribution by type of drink.

R Code

```
# Boxplot of sales by drink type
ggplot(cafe_sales, aes(x = Drink, y = Sold)) +
  geom_boxplot(fill = "#637D8D") +
  labs(title = "Drink Sales by Type (With Errors)")
```

Drink Sales by Type (With Errors)

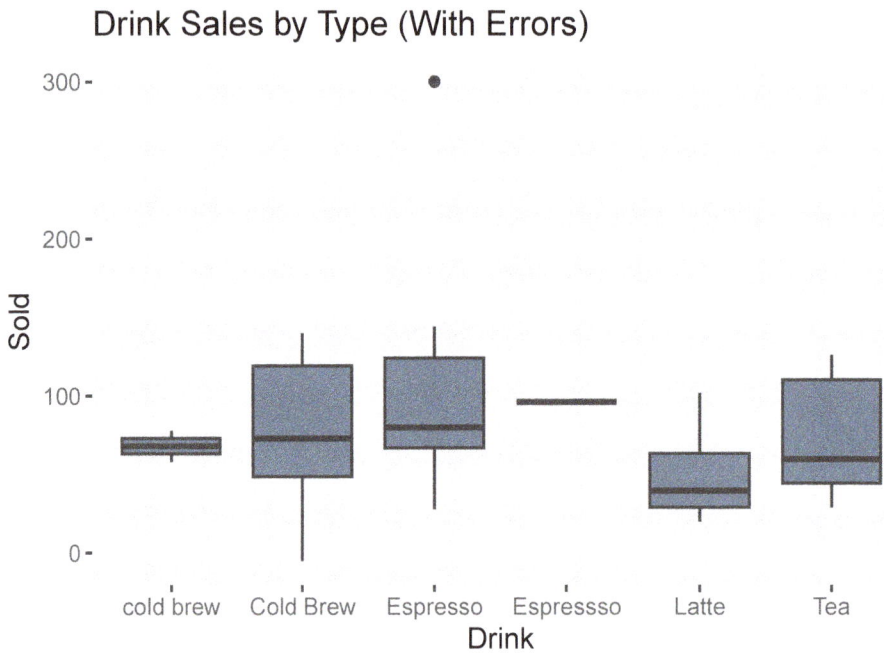

This chart lets you compare how sales vary by drink type. Any points outside the whiskers are considered outliers and may need further review. If you see multiple boxes for similar drink names (like "Espresso" and "Espressso"), this could indicate a spelling mistake that splits one category into two.

Wrap-Up

Graphs can quickly reveal problems in your dataset, such as missing values, inconsistent labels, or outliers that don't make sense. They are especially useful early in the data wrangling process because they help you spot issues that might not be obvious in raw tables or summaries. Once you identify a problem visually, you still need to go back and fix it using proper data cleaning functions in your code.

Exercises

Graphical Analytics in R

Data visualizations are one of the fastest ways to explore and clean messy datasets. In this exercise you will generate and analyze simulated datasets with intentional errors using R plots. You'll use line charts, scatterplots, histograms, and boxplots to detect issues such as missing data, unusual values, inconsistencies, and incorrect labels.

Dataset 1: Fitness Tracker Data (Steps and Heart Rate)

R Code

```
set.seed(101)

fitness_data <- data.frame(
  Date = seq.Date(
    from = as.Date("2024-07-01"),
    by = "day", length.out = 45
  ),
  Steps = sample(c(0, 1000:15000), 45, replace = TRUE),
  HeartRate = round(rnorm(45, mean = 70, sd = 10), 1)
)


# Unrealistic step count
fitness_data$Steps[5] <- 30000

# Very high heart rate
fitness_data$HeartRate[12] <- 200

# Missing heart rate value
fitness_data$HeartRate[25] <- NA

# Negative step count
fitness_data$Steps[40] <- -100

# Missing steps value
fitness_data$Steps[20] <- NA
```

1. Create a line chart of steps over time. What trends or problems do you observe?

2. Create a scatterplot of steps vs. heart rate. What anomalies or outliers

can you see?

3. Create a histogram of heart rate. Describe the distribution and any potential problems.

4. Use a boxplot of steps. Are there any outliers? What do they represent?

5. Check for missing values using a graph or other method. How many values are missing? Where are they?

Dataset 2: Student Exam Scores

R Code

```
set.seed(202)

exam_scores <- data.frame(
  StudentID = 1:50,
  Math = round(rnorm(50, mean = 78, sd = 10)),
  English = round(rnorm(50, mean = 72, sd = 12)),
  History = round(rnorm(50, mean = 70, sd = 15))
)


# Introduce errors
# Impossible Math scores: 110 and -10
exam_scores$Math[c(3, 17)] <- c(110, -10)

# Missing English score
exam_scores$English[25] <- NA

# Impossible History score: 200
exam_scores$History[45] <- 200

# Duplicate StudentID error
exam_scores$StudentID[10] <- 999
```

6. Create a histogram of Math scores. Do you see any scores that shouldn't be there?

7. Make a boxplot comparing scores across all three subjects. Which subject has the most variability or unusual values?

8. Create a scatterplot of Math vs. English scores. Do these two variables seem related? Any outliers?

9. Use a line chart to display scores by student ID. Which students stand out as having errors?

10. Plot missing data (using a trick or package like naniar if you want). Which variable has missing data? How might that affect analysis?

Dataset 3: Online Sales Orders

```
R Code
set.seed(303)

sales_data <- data.frame(
  OrderDate = seq.Date(as.Date("2024-08-01"),
    by = "day",
    length.out = 30
  ),
  UnitsSold = sample(c(1:80), 30, replace = TRUE),
  Category = sample(c(
    "Books", "Tech", "Clothes", "book",
    "TEch", "ClOthes"
  ), 30, replace = TRUE),
  Revenue = round(runif(30, 20, 300), 2)
)

# Add flaws
sales_data$UnitsSold[c(4, 12)] <- c(150, -5)
sales_data$Revenue[7] <- 0
sales_data$Revenue[15] <- NA
sales_data$Category[22] <- "Unknown"
```

11. Make a histogram of revenue. Are there any missing or zero values?

What do you notice?

12. Create a boxplot of revenue by category.What problems do you see with the categories?

13. Make a line chart of units sold over time.Do any sales figures stand out as errors?

14. Use a scatterplot of units sold versus revenue. Which data points would you investigate further?

15. Count how many unique categories are in the dataset. What needs to be fixed, and how would you do it?

Lab 8

Making Data Consistent

In input data, information is rarely clean or consistent. People enter text in different cases, dates get recorded in various formats, and measurements might use different units. These inconsistencies can lead to problems when you try to sort, filter, or analyze your data.

This lab shows how to standardize and clean inconsistent data. You'll learn how to clean up names and gender entries, unify date formats, handle numeric text, convert units like weight into a common format, and use frequency tables to catch lingering issues.

Lesson Steps

Step 1: Load packages and create the dataset

First, install and load the packages you'll need: tidyverse for data manipulation, lubridate for working with dates, janitor for quick tabulations, readr for parsing numbers, and stringr for working with text patterns.

R Code
```
# Install if not already installed

options(repos = c(CRAN = "https://cran.r-project.org"))
install.packages("tidyverse")
install.packages("lubridate")
install.packages("janitor")
install.packages("readr")
install.packages("stringr")

library(tidyverse)
library(lubridate)
library(janitor)
library(readr)
library(stringr)
```

Next, we create a small messy dataset that includes inconsistent names, gender labels, ages, dates, and weights.

R Code
```
data <- tibble(
  name = c("Alice", "ALICE", "Bob", "BOB", "Charlie"),
  gender = c("Male", "M", "female", "F", "FEMALE"),
  age = c("25", "twenty-five", "30", NA, "28"),
  order_date = c(
    "2023-01-01", "01/02/2023",
    "March 3, 2023", "Friday", NA
  ),
  weight = c("70kg", "154lbs", "72kg", "160 lb", "65kg")
)

data
```

Output
```
## # A tibble: 5 x 5
##    name    gender age         order_date     weight
##    <chr>   <chr>  <chr>       <chr>          <chr>
## 1 Alice    Male   25          2023-01-01     70kg
## 2 ALICE    M      twenty-five 01/02/2023     154lbs
## 3 Bob      female 30          March 3, 2023  72kg
## 4 BOB      F      <NA>        Friday         160 lb
## 5 Charlie  FEMALE 28          <NA>           65kg
```

Step 2: Standardize text columns

The name and gender columns are entered inconsistently. Some names are in uppercase, while others are not. Gender is recorded as "M," "F," "female," or other variations. These differences create problems when you try to group or summarize data. This is fixed by converting all names to title case using str_to_title() so every name looks like "Alice" instead of "ALICE." Then we use case_when() to convert various gender labels into just "Male" or "Female."

R Code
```
data$name <- str_to_title(data$name)

data$gender <- case_when(
   str_to_lower(data$gender) %in% c("male", "m") ~ "Male",
   str_to_lower(data$gender) %in% c("female", "f") ~ "Female",
   TRUE ~ data$gender
)

data
```

Output
```
## # A tibble: 5 x 5
##    name     gender age          order_date     weight
##    <chr>    <chr>  <chr>        <chr>          <chr>
## 1 Alice    Male   25           2023-01-01     70kg
## 2 Alice    Male   twenty-five  01/02/2023     154lbs
## 3 Bob      Female 30           March 3, 2023  72kg
## 4 Bob      Female <NA>         Friday         160 lb
## 5 Charlie  Female 28           <NA>           65kg
```

Step 3: Parse inconsistent dates

The order_date column contains dates in multiple formats. Some use dashes, others slashes, some are spelled out like "March 3, 2023," and one value is simply "Friday." When dates aren't consistent, it becomes impossible to sort or filter them reliably. We use parse_date_time() from the lubridate package to convert known formats into real date values. Any unrecognized entry becomes NA.

R Code
```
data$order_date_parsed <- parse_date_time(
  data$order_date,
  orders = c("ymd", "mdy", "B d, Y", "A")
)


data[, 1:4]
```

Output
```
## # A tibble: 5 x 4
##    name    gender age         order_date
##    <chr>   <chr>  <chr>       <chr>
## 1 Alice    Male   25          2023-01-01
## 2 Alice    Male   twenty-five 01/02/2023
## 3 Bob      Female 30          March 3, 2023
## 4 Bob      Female <NA>        Friday
## 5 Charlie  Female 28          <NA>
```

R Code
```
data[, 5:6]
```

Output
```
## # A tibble: 5 x 2
##    weight order_date_parsed
##    <chr>  <dttm>
## 1 70kg    2023-01-01 00:00:00
## 2 154lbs 2023-01-02 00:00:00
## 3 72kg    2023-03-03 00:00:00
## 4 160 lb 2025-07-29 00:00:00
## 5 65kg    NA
```

Step 4: Clean mixed-type numeric text

The age column includes numbers, text like "twenty-five," and missing values. R can't perform numeric operations if the values are stored as text. We use parse_number() from readr to extract any digits from the text. If it can't find a number, it returns NA. To keep the console clean, we wrap this in suppressWarnings().

R Code
```
data$age_num <- suppressWarnings(parse_number(data$age))

data[,1:4]
```

Output

```
## # A tibble: 5 x 4
##    name    gender age         order_date
##    <chr>   <chr>  <chr>       <chr>
## 1 Alice   Male   25          2023-01-01
## 2 Alice   Male   twenty-five 01/02/2023
## 3 Bob     Female 30          March 3, 2023
## 4 Bob     Female <NA>        Friday
## 5 Charlie Female 28          <NA>
```

R Code

```
data[,5:6]
```

Output

```
## # A tibble: 5 x 2
##    weight order_date_parsed
##    <chr>  <dttm>
## 1 70kg    2023-01-01 00:00:00
## 2 154lbs  2023-01-02 00:00:00
## 3 72kg    2023-03-03 00:00:00
## 4 160 lb  2025-07-29 00:00:00
## 5 65kg    NA
```

Step 5: Standardize units of measurement

The weight column mixes kilograms and pounds and includes text with the numbers. This inconsistency prevents comparison or calculation. To fix this first we extract the numeric value using parse_number(). Then we identify which entries use kilograms or pounds using str_detect(). Finally, we convert all values to kilograms using a conversion factor of 1 lb = 0.453592 kg.

```
R Code
data$weight_value <- parse_number(data$weight)

data$weight_unit <- ifelse(
  str_detect(data$weight, "kg"), "kg",
  ifelse(str_detect(data$weight, "lb|lbs"),
    "lb", NA_character_
  )
)

data$weight_kg <- ifelse(
  data$weight_unit == "kg", data$weight_value,
  ifelse(data$weight_unit == "lb",
    data$weight_value * 0.453592, NA_real_
  )
)


data[, 1:5]
```

Output

```
## # A tibble: 5 x 5
##   name     gender age           order_date    weight
##   <chr>    <chr>  <chr>         <chr>         <chr>
## 1 Alice    Male   25            2023-01-01    70kg
## 2 Alice    Male   twenty-five   01/02/2023    154lbs
## 3 Bob      Female 30            March 3, 2023 72kg
## 4 Bob      Female <NA>          Friday        160 lb
## 5 Charlie  Female 28            <NA>          65kg
```

R Code

```
data[, 6:9]
```

Output

```
## # A tibble: 5 x 4
##   order_date_parsed   age_num weight_value weight_unit
##   <dttm>                <dbl>        <dbl> <chr>
## 1 2023-01-01 00:00:00      25           70 kg
## 2 2023-01-02 00:00:00      NA          154 lb
## 3 2023-03-03 00:00:00      30           72 kg
## 4 2025-07-29 00:00:00      NA          160 lb
## 5 NA                       28           65 kg
```

Step 6: Use frequency tables to check for inconsistencies

Even after cleaning, it's helpful to double-check your work. Frequency tables let you quickly see all unique values and how often they appear. This can help catch typos or values that didn't get cleaned. We use tabyl() from janitor to summarize the gender column, and count() from dplyr to view the original order_date column.

R Code
```
tabyl(data$gender)
```

Output
```
##   data$gender n percent
##        Female 3     0.6
##          Male 2     0.4
```

R Code
```
count(data, order_date)
```

Output

```
## # A tibble: 5 x 2
##    order_date        n
##    <chr>         <int>
## 1 01/02/2023        1
## 2 2023-01-01        1
## 3 Friday            1
## 4 March 3, 2023     1
## 5 <NA>              1
```

Wrap-up

In this lab, you cleaned and standardized a dataset with inconsistent text, mixed numeric formats, and conflicting units. You used string tools to fix names and gender labels, handled multiple date formats with parse_date_time(), extracted numeric values from text with parse_number(), and converted all weights into kilograms. Finally, you used frequency tables to spot any issues that remained.

Exercises

Making Data Consistent

This set of exercises will give you practice identifying and fixing inconsistent data values to ensure your dataset is clean, standardized, and ready for analysis.

Dataset: School Event Registrations

R Code

```
library(tidyverse)
library(lubridate)
library(janitor)
library(readr)
library(stringr)

registrations <- tibble(
  student_name = c(
    "  o'connor, mary  ", "Lee,David",
    "Nguyen - Amy", "  ali Hasan",
    "SINGH; Priya"
  ),
  sex = c("fem", "M", "FEMALE", "MALE", "n/a"),
  grad_year = c(
    "2026", "twenty twenty-five", "2024",
    NA, "2025"
  ),
  sign_up = c(
    "2024.04.10", "10-04-2024", "April 10 2024",
    "next Monday", ""
  ),
  height_recorded = c(
    "160 cm", "5ft6", "63 in", "1.65m",
    "five foot five"
  )
)
```

1. Clean the student_name column to remove leading/trailing spaces and standardize to Title Case format without punctuation (e.g., "Mary Oconnor"). Then count how many unique names remain.

2. Separate names into first and last name columns using patterns like comma, hyphen, semicolon, or space. Are any full names missing either a first or last part?

3. Combine the cleaned names into a new column clean_name in the format "First Last."

4. Recode the sex column into standard labels: `"Male"`, `"Female"`, or `"Unknown"`. Use str_to_lower() and case_when(). List the recoded frequencies using tabyl().

5. What percentage of entries were labeled "Unknown"?

6. Extract numeric values from grad_year using parse_number() and store in grad_numeric.

7. Which value could not be parsed? Replace it with 2025 manually in the new column.

8. Calculate how many students are expected to graduate before the year 2025.

9. Use parse_date_time() on sign_up using formats "ymd", "dmy", "B d Y", "A". How many sign-up dates successfully convert to valid Date values?

10. List any original sign_up values that failed to convert.

11. Use parse_number() to extract the numeric part of height_recorded into a new column height_num.

12. Create a height_unit column:

- `"cm"` for values with `"cm"`
- `"in"` for values with `"in"` or `"foot"`
- `"m"` for values with `"m"` (but not `"cm"`)
- Otherwise `"unknown"`

13. Convert all heights to centimeters in a new column height_cm:

    - 1 inch = 2.54 cm
    - 1 meter = 100 cm
    - 1 foot = 12 inches

14. Which row had an unclear or missing height unit?

15. Show a cleaned version of the dataset with: clean_name, sex, grad_numeric, signup_parsed, and height_cm. How many complete rows remain?

Lab 9

Accuracy and Validity

Inaccurate or invalid data can seriously mislead your analysis. Accuracy means the data correctly reflects real-world values. Validity means the data falls within acceptable or expected ranges. Both are essential for meaningful, reliable insights.

In this lab, we'll use a small simulated dataset to explore common issues that affect accuracy and validity—like outliers, impossible values, logic conflicts between columns, and mismatches in calculated fields. We'll walk through each type of issue and use R to detect and flag problems so we can begin to fix them.

Lesson Steps

Step 1: Create and View the Dataset

We'll start by creating a messy dataset with several intentional accuracy problems. Some ages are unrealistic, some wage and hour totals don't line up, and there are logical problems in the birth and death dates.

R Code

```
data <- data.frame(
  ID = 1:8,
  Age = c(25, 32, 45, -5, 120, 35, 60, 28),
  Score = c(78, 88, 90, 100, 110, 40, 95, 85),
  Color = c(
    "Blue", "Red", "Green", "Toilet Paper",
    "Blue", "Green", "Red", "Green"
  ),
  BirthDate = as.Date(c(
    "1990-01-01", "1988-04-10",
    "1975-06-30", "2000-10-05", "1900-01-01", "1985-09-17",
    "1960-03-22", "1995-07-12"
  )),
  DeathDate = as.Date(c(
    "2020-01-01", NA, NA, NA, "1990-01-01",
    NA, "2022-12-31", NA
  )),
  Wage = c(20, 25, 30, 20, 20, 18, 30, 28),
  Hours = c(40, 40, 40, 40, 40, 35, 40, 40),
  WeeklyPay = c(
    800, 1000, 1200, 800, 950, 630,
    1300, 1120
  )
)

data[, 1:5]
```

Output

```
##    ID Age Score          Color  BirthDate
## 1   1  25    78           Blue 1990-01-01
## 2   2  32    88            Red 1988-04-10
## 3   3  45    90          Green 1975-06-30
## 4   4  -5   100 Toilet Paper 2000-10-05
## 5   5 120   110           Blue 1900-01-01
## 6   6  35    40          Green 1985-09-17
## 7   7  60    95            Red 1960-03-22
## 8   8  28    85          Green 1995-07-12
```

R Code

```
data[, 6:9]
```

Output

```
##    DeathDate Wage Hours WeeklyPay
## 1 2020-01-01   20    40       800
## 2       <NA>   25    40      1000
## 3       <NA>   30    40      1200
## 4       <NA>   20    40       800
## 5 1990-01-01   20    40       950
## 6       <NA>   18    35       630
## 7 2022-12-31   30    40      1300
## 8       <NA>   28    40      1120
```

Step 2: Identify Outliers with Boxplots

One way to check for accuracy issues is to look for outliers—values that are unusually high or low compared to the rest. Outliers can sometimes signal errors or unusual data entries.

We can use a simple boxplot to visually identify outliers in numeric columns.

R Code
```
boxplot(data$Age)
```

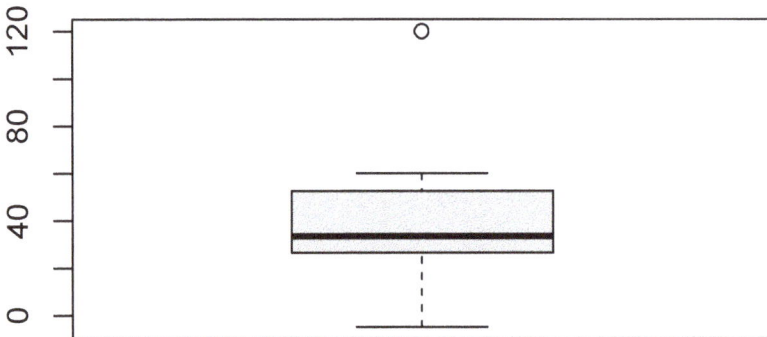

This shows a clear outlier: one value (-5) is outside the normal age range. This suggests an error that needs review.

Step 3: Use Z-Scores to Spot Outliers

Z-scores measure how many standard deviations a value is from the mean. They can help identify numeric outliers statistically, not just visually.

R Code
```
z_scores <- scale(data$Age)

# Flags values more than 2 SDs away

which(abs(z_scores) > 2)
```

Output
```
## [1] 5
```

This will return any rows where the age is unusually far from the average. In this case, integer(0) means there are no z-score outliers beyond 2 standard deviations, but visual inspection still flagged -5 as suspicious.

Step 4: Investigate Data Range Issues

It's important to summarize and inspect the full range of values in your numeric columns to look for unrealistic or invalid values. For example, an age of -5 is not valid, and a test score above 100 may not be allowed.

R Code
```
summary(data$Age)
```

Output
```
##     Min. 1st Qu.  Median    Mean 3rd Qu.     Max.
##    -5.00   27.25   33.50   42.50   48.75  120.00
```

R Code
```
range(data$Score)
```

Output
```
## [1]   40 110
```

This tells us the age column ranges from -5 to 120 and scores range from 40 to 110. Depending on your context, ages below 0 and scores above 100 may be invalid and need correction.

Step 5: Use Conditional Logic to Flag Bad Values

You can create new columns that label whether each value passes or fails a condition. This helps flag issues clearly and automatically.

For example, let's flag unrealistic ages.

R Code
```
data$AgeFlag <- ifelse(data$Age < 0 | data$Age > 100,
  "Out of Range", "OK"
)
data[, 1:5]
```

Output

```
##    ID Age Score        Color  BirthDate
## 1  1  25   78          Blue   1990-01-01
## 2  2  32   88           Red   1988-04-10
## 3  3  45   90         Green   1975-06-30
## 4  4  -5  100 Toilet Paper    2000-10-05
## 5  5 120  110          Blue   1900-01-01
## 6  6  35   40         Green   1985-09-17
## 7  7  60   95           Red   1960-03-22
## 8  8  28   85         Green   1995-07-12
```

R Code

```
data[, 6:10]
```

Output

```
##     DeathDate Wage Hours WeeklyPay       AgeFlag
## 1 2020-01-01   20    40       800            OK
## 2       <NA>   25    40      1000            OK
## 3       <NA>   30    40      1200            OK
## 4       <NA>   20    40       800 Out of Range
## 5 1990-01-01   20    40       950 Out of Range
## 6       <NA>   18    35       630            OK
## 7 2022-12-31   30    40      1300            OK
## 8       <NA>   28    40      1120            OK
```

This adds a new column to show whether each age entry falls outside a reasonable human range.

Step 6: Check Set Membership for Categorical Values

In categorical columns, it's common to see unexpected or incorrect values. To check for this, we compare the values in the column to a set of accepted choices.

R Code
```
cat(paste(unique(data$Color), collapse = "\n"))
```

Output
```
## Blue
## Red
## Green
## Toilet Paper
```

R Code
```
# Define valid color options

valid_colors <- c("Red", "Blue", "Green")

# Flag invalid color entries

data$ColorValid <- data$Color %in% valid_colors
data[,1:6]
```

Output

```
##    ID Age Score          Color  BirthDate  DeathDate
## 1   1  25    78           Blue 1990-01-01 2020-01-01
## 2   2  32    88            Red 1988-04-10       <NA>
## 3   3  45    90          Green 1975-06-30       <NA>
## 4   4  -5   100 Toilet Paper 2000-10-05       <NA>
## 5   5 120   110           Blue 1900-01-01 1990-01-01
## 6   6  35    40          Green 1985-09-17       <NA>
## 7   7  60    95            Red 1960-03-22 2022-12-31
## 8   8  28    85          Green 1995-07-12       <NA>
```

R Code

```
data[,7:10]
```

Output

```
##    Wage Hours WeeklyPay      AgeFlag
## 1    20    40       800           OK
## 2    25    40      1000           OK
## 3    30    40      1200           OK
## 4    20    40       800 Out of Range
## 5    20    40       950 Out of Range
## 6    18    35       630           OK
## 7    30    40      1300           OK
## 8    28    40      1120           OK
```

This shows that one row includes "Toilet Paper" as a color, which clearly doesn't belong and was likely a data entry mistake.

Step 7: Apply Cross-Field Validation Rules

Sometimes individual values seem fine, but don't make sense when combined with values in related fields. For example, someone's death date should not come before their birth date.

R Code
```
data$DeathBeforeBirth <- data$DeathDate < data$BirthDate
data[,1:6]
```

Output
```
##   ID Age Score         Color  BirthDate  DeathDate
## 1  1  25    78          Blue 1990-01-01 2020-01-01
## 2  2  32    88           Red 1988-04-10       <NA>
## 3  3  45    90         Green 1975-06-30       <NA>
## 4  4  -5   100 Toilet Paper 2000-10-05       <NA>
## 5  5 120   110          Blue 1900-01-01 1990-01-01
## 6  6  35    40         Green 1985-09-17       <NA>
## 7  7  60    95           Red 1960-03-22 2022-12-31
## 8  8  28    85         Green 1995-07-12       <NA>
```

R Code
```
data[,7:11]
```

Output

```
##    Wage Hours WeeklyPay      AgeFlag ColorValid
## 1    20    40       800          OK       TRUE
## 2    25    40      1000          OK       TRUE
## 3    30    40      1200          OK       TRUE
## 4    20    40       800 Out of Range      FALSE
## 5    20    40       950 Out of Range       TRUE
## 6    18    35       630          OK       TRUE
## 7    30    40      1300          OK       TRUE
## 8    28    40      1120          OK       TRUE
```

This comparison flags rows where death occurs before birth. Logical errors like these often indicate incorrect or swapped data entries.

Step 8: Check Calculated Fields for Mismatches

When one column is meant to be derived from others, it's smart to recalculate the expected value and compare. For example, WeeklyPay should equal Wage × Hours.

R Code

```
data$ExpectedPay <- data$Wage * data$Hours
data$PayCheck <- ifelse(data$WeeklyPay == data$ExpectedPay,
  "Match", "Mismatch"
)
data[, 1:5]
```

Output

```
##    ID Age Score          Color  BirthDate
## 1   1  25    78           Blue 1990-01-01
## 2   2  32    88            Red 1988-04-10
## 3   3  45    90          Green 1975-06-30
## 4   4  -5   100 Toilet Paper 2000-10-05
## 5   5 120   110           Blue 1900-01-01
## 6   6  35    40          Green 1985-09-17
## 7   7  60    95            Red 1960-03-22
## 8   8  28    85          Green 1995-07-12
```

R Code

```
data[, 5:10]
```

Output

```
##     BirthDate  DeathDate Wage Hours WeeklyPay       AgeFlag
## 1 1990-01-01 2020-01-01   20    40       800            OK
## 2 1988-04-10       <NA>   25    40      1000            OK
## 3 1975-06-30       <NA>   30    40      1200            OK
## 4 2000-10-05       <NA>   20    40       800 Out of Range
## 5 1900-01-01 1990-01-01   20    40       950 Out of Range
## 6 1985-09-17       <NA>   18    35       630            OK
## 7 1960-03-22 2022-12-31   30    40      1300            OK
## 8 1995-07-12       <NA>   28    40      1120            OK
```

R Code

```
data[, 11:14]
```

Output

```
##    ColorValid DeathBeforeBirth ExpectedPay PayCheck
## 1       TRUE            FALSE          800    Match
## 2       TRUE               NA         1000    Match
## 3       TRUE               NA         1200    Match
## 4      FALSE               NA          800    Match
## 5       TRUE            FALSE          800 Mismatch
## 6       TRUE               NA          630    Match
## 7       TRUE            FALSE         1200 Mismatch
## 8       TRUE               NA         1120    Match
```

Now you can easily see whether the pay values match what we'd expect based on wage and hours. Any mismatch could indicate a data entry error.

Wrap-Up

In this lab, you explored several methods to assess and improve the accuracy and validity of your data. You learned how to use boxplots and z-scores to identify outliers, and how to flag unrealistic values by applying conditional logic. Additionally, you checked whether values fell within valid sets and verified logical consistency across related fields, such as dates. Recalculating and validating computed fields was another important step to ensure correctness.

Exercises

Detecting Invalid or Inaccurate Data

Now that you've learned how to identify outliers, invalid values, and logic errors, it's time to apply your skills to new datasets. In this exercise, you'll work with three different datasets that contain accuracy or validity problems. Use your understanding of summary statistics, visualizations, logical conditions, and cross-field checks to detect and describe the issues.

Dataset 1: Customer Transactions

This dataset tracks purchases made by customers, including an unrealistic age, a suspicious discount, and logic issues between quantity and total cost.

```
R Code
customers <- data.frame(
  CustID = 101:108,
  Age = c(34, 45, 27, 150, -3, 40, 29, 38),
  Quantity = c(2, 1, 5, 3, 10, 1, 2, 4),
  UnitPrice = c(25, 100, 10, 30, 15, 20, 50, 40),
  TotalPrice = c(
    50, 100, 50, 100, 120, 18,
    100, 170
  ),
  DiscountCode = c(
    "SUMMER10", "SAVE20", "XMAS",
    "INVALID", "NONE", "XMAS", "SAVE20", "TOILET"
  )
)
```

1. Create a boxplot of Age. What value(s) look unrealistic?

2. Use a logical condition to flag customers with age below 0 or above 100.

3. Check whether each TotalPrice is equal to Quantity * UnitPrice. How many mismatches are there?

4. List all unique values in the DiscountCode column. Which seem invalid?

5. Create a logical column to flag whether each discount code is from a valid set: "SUMMER10", "SAVE20", "XMAS", "NONE".

Dataset 2: Patient Vitals

This dataset tracks blood pressure and temperature readings. Some values are outside biological norms, and there's an inconsistency between systolic and diastolic readings.

R Code

```
vitals <- data.frame(
  PatientID = 201:208,
  Systolic = c(
    120, 130, 110, 90, 250, 300, 135, 100
  ),
  Diastolic = c(
    80, 85, 70, 60, 90, 150, 60, 95
  ),
  TempF = c(
    98.6, 99.1, 102.5, 94.0, 110.0,
    96.0, 97.8, 98.0
  ),
  VisitDate = as.Date(c(
    "2023-01-01", "2023-01-05",   "2023-01-10",
    "2023-02-01", "2023-02-03",   "2023-03-01",
    "2023-03-15", "2023-03-20"
  ))
)
```

6. Use summary() to examine the TempF column. Which values appear outside the expected body temperature range (95–105° F)?

7. Create a logical column flagging any temperatures above 105 or below 95 as out of range.

8. Add a column flagging whether Systolic is less than Diastolic. Is this ever true?

9. Use a boxplot to visualize Systolic and identify any outliers.

10. How many patients have a systolic pressure greater than 200 or a diastolic pressure above 120?

Dataset 3: Student Submissions

This dataset includes problems with timestamps, missing values, and mismatched calculations.

```
R Code
submissions <- data.frame(
  StudentID = 301:308,
  SubmitTime = as.POSIXct(c(
    "2025-06-10 10:00", "2025-06-11 14:30",
    NA, "2025-06-12 09:00",
    "2025-06-10 08:00",
    "2025-06-15 23:59",
    "2025-06-13 12:00",
    "2025-06-09 20:00"
  )),
  Deadline = as.POSIXct(rep("2025-06-12 23:59", 8)),
  Pages = c(5, 6, 7, 8, 5, 3, NA, 10),
  WordsPerPage = c(
    250, 300, 250, 200, 300,
    275, 250, 275
  ),
  WordCount = c(
    1250, 1800, 1700, 1500, 1600,
    800, 1200, 2500
  )
)
```

11. Count how many rows have a missing SubmitTime or Pages.

12. Add a new column LateFlag indicating whether a submission was past the deadline.

13. Create a new column ExpectedWords as Pages * WordsPerPage. How many rows mismatch the actual WordCount?

14. Identify any students with a Pages count over 10. Are there any?

15. Create a logical column flagging entries with missing or mismatched information across any key field.

Lab 10

Ensuring Uniqueness

Uniqueness means that certain fields in your dataset—like ID numbers or email addresses—should appear only once. When these values are repeated, it can signal problems like accidental duplication, bad joins, or copy-paste errors. If you don't catch these issues, you might double-count people, miscalculate totals, or run into trouble when merging datasets. In this lab, we'll walk through how to detect, understand, and handle duplicate records.

Lesson Steps

Step 1: Create the Dataset

We'll simulate a small dataset with some intentional problems. Some rows are full duplicates, and some IDs are reused. These issues will help us practice checking for uniqueness and exploring whether repeated rows are true duplicates or legitimate repeated actions.

R Code

```
# Install if not already installed


options(repos = c(CRAN = "https://cran.r-project.org"))
install.packages('deplyr')
library(dplyr)
```

R Code

```
# Simulate sales data

data <- tibble::tibble(
  CustomerID = c(101, 102, 102, 103, 104, 105, 106, 106, 106),
  Name = c(
    "Jane Smith", "Tom Lee", "Tom Lee", "Sam King",
    "Ada Ray", "Liam Dee", "Noah Fox", "Noah Fox",
    "Noah Fox"
  ),
  Purchase = c(180, 250, 250, 300, 180, 150, 180, 180, 180),
  Date = as.Date(c(
    "2023-05-01", "2023-05-01", "2023-05-01",
    "2023-06-01", "2023-06-03", "2023-06-03",
    "2023-06-05", "2023-06-05", "2023-06-05"
  ))
)

data
```

Output

```
## # A tibble: 9 x 4
##    CustomerID Name       Purchase Date
##         <dbl> <chr>          <dbl> <date>
## 1        101 Jane Smith       180 2023-05-01
## 2        102 Tom Lee          250 2023-05-01
## 3        102 Tom Lee          250 2023-05-01
## 4        103 Sam King         300 2023-06-01
## 5        104 Ada Ray          180 2023-06-03
## 6        105 Liam Dee         150 2023-06-03
## 7        106 Noah Fox         180 2023-06-05
## 8        106 Noah Fox         180 2023-06-05
## 9        106 Noah Fox         180 2023-06-05
```

Step 2: Detect Duplicated Rows

To check for duplicated records, we use the duplicated() function. This returns a logical vector showing which rows are exact repeats.

R Code

```
duplicated(data)
```

Output

```
## [1] FALSE FALSE  TRUE FALSE FALSE FALSE FALSE  TRUE  TRUE
```

R Code

```
data[duplicated(data), ]
```

Output

```
## # A tibble: 3 x 4
##    CustomerID Name      Purchase Date
##         <dbl> <chr>        <dbl> <date>
## 1         102 Tom Lee        250 2023-05-01
## 2         106 Noah Fox       180 2023-06-05
## 3         106 Noah Fox       180 2023-06-05
```

In our dataset, this check returns three duplicate rows. Exact duplicates should be removed, but only if we're sure they're unintentional. Always review them carefully.

Step 3: Understand What Causes Duplicates

Duplicates can happen for lots of reasons. You might accidentally copy-paste a record twice, or a system might sync the same row multiple times. A very common reason is joining datasets incorrectly—especially when both tables have repeated values for the same ID.

Let's simulate a bad join that creates duplicates.

R Code
```r
# Simulated sales and customer info tables

sales <- tibble(CustomerID = c(101, 102, 102))
customer_info <- tibble(
  CustomerID = c(102, 102),
  Name = c("Tom Lee", "Tom Lee")
)

# Perform a left join

bad_join <- left_join(sales, customer_info,
  by = "CustomerID"
)

bad_join
```

Output
```
## # A tibble: 5 x 2
##    CustomerID Name
##         <dbl> <chr>
## 1         101 <NA>
## 2         102 Tom Lee
## 3         102 Tom Lee
## 4         102 Tom Lee
## 5         102 Tom Lee
```

This kind of many-to-many join can multiply rows. For CustomerID 102, we now have multiple combinations of the same person. This inflates your data and can cause huge problems in analysis.

Step 4: Distinguish Duplicates from Repeats

Just because a value appears more than once doesn't mean it's wrong. If a customer bought more than once, you'll have multiple rows for that person. That's a legitimate repeat, not a mistake.

To explore this, we can filter all rows for a specific customer:

R Code
```
filter(data, CustomerID == 102)
```

Output
```
## # A tibble: 2 x 4
##    CustomerID Name     Purchase Date
##         <dbl> <chr>        <dbl> <date>
## 1         102 Tom Lee        250 2023-05-01
## 2         102 Tom Lee        250 2023-05-01
```

These two rows are identical. But without more context—like a transaction ID or timestamp—it's hard to know if they reflect two real purchases or a mistaken duplicate.

Step 5: Use Frequency Tables

To see which customers show up more than once, we can count how often each combination of ID and name appears. This gives us a better picture of repeated entries.

R Code

```
arrange(count(data, CustomerID, Name), desc(n))
```

Output

```
## # A tibble: 6 x 3
##    CustomerID Name             n
##         <dbl> <chr>        <int>
## 1         106 Noah Fox         3
## 2         102 Tom Lee          2
## 3         101 Jane Smith       1
## 4         103 Sam King         1
## 5         104 Ada Ray          1
## 6         105 Liam Dee         1
```

This tells us who appears most often. If a customer shows up 3+ times with the same details, that might be suspicious. But again, frequency alone doesn't confirm whether repeats are valid or not.

Step 6: Check for Unique IDs

Some fields—like CustomerID—are supposed to be unique. If they're not, your joins and groupings may break. This quick check tells us whether IDs are duplicated:

R Code

```
any(duplicated(data$CustomerID))
```

Output

```
## [1] TRUE
```

The result [1] TRUE means at least one CustomerID appears more than once. If these IDs are meant to identify a unique person, this could distort analysis results.

Step 7: Remove or Flag Duplicates

Once you've identified true duplicate rows, you can remove them using distinct(). But sometimes, it's safer to flag possible duplicates rather than deleting them.

R Code

```
# Remove exact duplicates


data_unique <- distinct(data)


# Flag possible duplicate records based on selected fields
data_grouped <- group_by(data, CustomerID, Name, Purchase)
data_mutated <- mutate(data_grouped, Flag = ifelse(n() > 1,
                                 "Possible Duplicate", "OK"))
data_flagged <- ungroup(data_mutated)


data_flagged[,1:3]
```

Output

```
## # A tibble: 9 x 3
##    CustomerID Name        Purchase
##         <dbl> <chr>          <dbl>
## 1         101 Jane Smith       180
## 2         102 Tom Lee          250
## 3         102 Tom Lee          250
## 4         103 Sam King         300
## 5         104 Ada Ray          180
## 6         105 Liam Dee         150
## 7         106 Noah Fox         180
## 8         106 Noah Fox         180
## 9         106 Noah Fox         180
```

R Code

```
data_flagged[,4:5]
```

133

```
Output
## # A tibble: 9 x 2
##   Date        Flag
##   <date>      <chr>
## 1 2023-05-01 OK
## 2 2023-05-01 Possible Duplicate
## 3 2023-05-01 Possible Duplicate
## 4 2023-06-01 OK
## 5 2023-06-03 OK
## 6 2023-06-03 OK
## 7 2023-06-05 Possible Duplicate
## 8 2023-06-05 Possible Duplicate
## 9 2023-06-05 Possible Duplicate
```

This method preserves the full dataset but clearly marks rows that may need review.

Wrap-Up

In this lab, you learned how to ensure uniqueness in your data, focusing especially on key fields like IDs. You practiced detecting exact duplicates using functions like duplicated(), and gained insight into common causes of duplicates such as bad joins or data entry errors. It was important to distinguish true duplicates from valid repeated actions by examining the context. You also used frequency counts to identify suspicious patterns and checked the uniqueness of IDs to maintain data integrity. Finally, you learned how to safely remove or flag duplicate records. It is always important to carefully investigate repeated values before deciding if they are errors.

Exercises

Finding and Fixing Duplicate Records

Now that you've explored how to detect duplicates, distinguish real repetitions from errors, and flag or remove problematic entries, it's time to apply these skills. In this exercise, you'll investigate uniqueness violations in a series of datasets. These tasks will help reinforce how to validate ID fields, manage join errors, and flag questionable rows without immediately deleting them.

Dataset 1: Event Registrations

This dataset simulates online registrations for a conference. Some entries are duplicates or reused email addresses, and there are no unique IDs.

R Code

```
registrations <- tibble::tibble(
  Name = c(
    "Alice Chen", "Bob Ray", "Alice Chen", "Dana Liu",
    "Carlos Mendez", "Bob Ray", "Eva Ford", "Alice Chen"
  ),
  Email = c(
    "alice@gmail.com", "bob@yahoo.com", "alice@gmail.com",
    "dana@uni.edu", "carlos@company.com", "bob@yahoo.com",
    "eva@school.edu", "alice@gmail.com"
  ),
  TicketType = c(
    "General", "Student", "General", "VIP",
    "General", "Student", "Student", "General"
  )
)
```

1. Use duplicated() to find exact duplicate rows. How many are there?

2. Count how many times each Email appears. Which addresses appear more than once?

3. Create a logical column flagging rows where Email is duplicated.

4. Use distinct() to remove full duplicates. What is the new number of rows?

5. Why might it be risky to delete all duplicate Email entries without checking the full context?

Dataset 2: Orders and Products

This dataset simulates a bad join between two tables: one of orders and one of products. You'll explore how repeating keys can lead to row inflation and duplication errors.

```
R Code
orders <- tibble::tibble(
  OrderID = c(201, 202, 203),
  ProductID = c(1, 2, 2)
)


products <- tibble::tibble(
  ProductID = c(2, 2),
  ProductName = c("Notebook", "Notebook")
)


joined_data <- left_join(orders, products, by = "ProductID")
```

6. What happens to the number of rows after the join? Why?

7. Which key field caused the duplication during the join?

8. Use duplicated() on the OrderID column in the 'joined_data. Are any OrderID s repeated?

9. Is the repetition a real data problem, or just an artifact of the join? Explain.

10. What could you add to the original tables to make the join behave better?

Dataset 3: Survey Submissions

This dataset contains responses to a short survey. It includes respondent IDs and a timestamp. You'll examine possible ID reuse and submission errors.

```
R Code
survey <- tibble::tibble(
  RespondentID = c(1, 2, 2, 3, 4, 5, 5, 5),
  Timestamp = as.POSIXct(c(
    "2025-06-01 09:00", "2025-06-01 10:00",
    "2025-06-01 10:01", "2025-06-01 11:00",
    "2025-06-01 12:00", "2025-06-01 13:00",
    "2025-06-01 13:01", "2025-06-01 13:02"
  )),
  Rating = c(5, 4, 4, 3, 5, 2, 2, 2)
)
```

11. How many rows reuse the same RespondentID?

12. Create a frequency table of RespondentID using count(). Which ID appears most?

13. Use group_by() and mutate() to add a flag column for n() > 1 repeats by RespondentID.

14. What might be a legitimate reason for multiple rows per respondent in this dataset?

15. What kind of column could help distinguish valid repeat entries from duplicates?

Lab 11

Completion

Handling missing or incomplete data is a key part of data wrangling because real-world datasets often have gaps or absent values. Data completion involves identifying, managing, and filling these missing parts to ensure your dataset is accurate and reliable for analysis. Proper handling prevents bias and improves insights. Common approaches include removing missing entries, imputing values, or joining with reference data.

Lesson Steps

Step 1: Create Dataset with Missing and Incomplete Data

We start by simulating a dataset with deliberate missing values in various columns.

R Code
```
# Install if not already installed


options(repos = c(CRAN = "https://cran.r-project.org"))
install.packages('tidyverse')
library(tidyverse)
```

R Code
```
students <- tibble::tibble(
  StudentID = 1:8,
  Name = c(
    "Alice", "Bob", "Carlos", "Dana", "Eva",
    NA, "George", "Helen"
  ),
  Age = c(14, 15, NA, 14, 13, 14, NA, 15),
  Grade = c(9, 9, 9, NA, 8, 9, 9, 9),
  ZIP = c(
    "10001", NA, "30301", "60601",
    NA, "33101", NA, "90001"
  )
)
students
```

Output

```
## # A tibble: 8 x 5
##    StudentID Name     Age Grade ZIP
##        <int> <chr>  <dbl> <dbl> <chr>
## 1          1 Alice     14     9 10001
## 2          2 Bob       15     9 <NA>
## 3          3 Carlos    NA     9 30301
## 4          4 Dana      14    NA 60601
## 5          5 Eva       13     8 <NA>
## 6          6 <NA>      14     9 33101
## 7          7 George    NA     9 <NA>
## 8          8 Helen     15     9 90001
```

Step 2: Identify Missing Data

Missing data are values absent or recorded as NA. Incomplete data have some fields partially filled. To examine missing values, use summary() and colSums(is.na()).

R Code

```
summary(students[,1:3])
```

141

Output

```
##     StudentID          Name                    Age
##   Min.   :1.00    Length:8          Min.    :13.00
##   1st Qu.:2.75    Class :character  1st Qu.:14.00
##   Median :4.50    Mode  :character  Median :14.00
##   Mean   :4.50                      Mean    :14.17
##   3rd Qu.:6.25                      3rd Qu.:14.75
##   Max.   :8.00                      Max.    :15.00
##                                     NA's    :2
```

R Code

```
summary(students[,4:5])
```

Output

```
##       Grade            ZIP
##   Min.    :8.000   Length:8
##   1st Qu.:9.000    Class :character
##   Median :9.000    Mode  :character
##   Mean    :8.857
##   3rd Qu.:9.000
##   Max.    :9.000
##   NA's    :1
```

R Code

```
colSums(is.na(students))
```

Output

## StudentID	Name	Age	Grade	ZIP
## 0	1	2	1	3

Function summary() shows basic stats and missing counts for numeric columns. The colSums(is.na()) counts missing values across all columns, including character fields.

Step 3: Strategies to Handle Missing Data - Omit Missing Values

Remove rows with missing values using drop_na(). This works best if missingness is minimal and random.

R Code
```
library(tidyr)

students_cleaned <- drop_na(students)
students_cleaned
```

Output
```
## # A tibble: 2 x 5
##    StudentID Name    Age Grade ZIP
##        <int> <chr> <dbl> <dbl> <chr>
## 1          1 Alice    14     9 10001
## 2          8 Helen    15     9 90001
```

Note: This may drop many rows if missingness is widespread.

Step 4: Strategies to Handle Missing Data - Impute Values Thoughtfully

Fill missing values using logical rules based on domain knowledge. For example, set missing age to 14 if grade is 9.

```
R Code
library(dplyr)

students_imputed <- mutate(
  students,
  Age = if_else(is.na(Age) & Grade == 9, 14, Age)
)
students_imputed
```

```
Output
## # A tibble: 8 x 5
##    StudentID Name      Age Grade ZIP
##        <int> <chr>   <dbl> <dbl> <chr>
## 1          1 Alice      14     9 10001
## 2          2 Bob        15     9 <NA>
## 3          3 Carlos     14     9 30301
## 4          4 Dana       14    NA 60601
## 5          5 Eva        13     8 <NA>
## 6          6 <NA>       14     9 33101
## 7          7 George     14     9 <NA>
## 8          8 Helen      15     9 90001
```

Step 5: Strategies to Handle Missing Data - Use Filler Values Only When Appropriate

Replace missing values with fillers like 0 only if it makes logical sense.

```
R Code
meat_data <- tibble(
  Person = c("A", "B", "C", "D"),
  MeatMealsPerWeek = c(3, 7, NA, 0)
)


meat_data2 <- mutate(
  meat_data,
  MeatMealsPerWeek = replace_na(MeatMealsPerWeek, 0)
)
meat_data2
```

```
Output
## # A tibble: 4 x 2
##    Person MeatMealsPerWeek
##    <chr>             <dbl>
## 1 A                     3
## 2 B                     7
## 3 C                     0
## 4 D                     0
```

Step 6: Completing Incomplete Data Using Joins

For incomplete data where some fields are missing but keys exist (e.g., ZIP codes), enrich your dataset by joining with a reference table.

R Code
```
zip_ref <- tibble(
  ZIP = c("10001", "30301", "60601", "33101", "90001"),
  State = c("NY", "GA", "IL", "FL", "CA")
)


students_completed <- left_join(students,
  zip_ref,
  by = "ZIP"
)
students_completed
```

Output
```
## # A tibble: 8 x 6
##    StudentID Name    Age Grade ZIP   State
##        <int> <chr> <dbl> <dbl> <chr> <chr>
## 1          1 Alice    14     9 10001 NY
## 2          2 Bob      15     9 <NA>  <NA>
## 3          3 Carlos   NA     9 30301 GA
## 4          4 Dana     14    NA 60601 IL
## 5          5 Eva      13     8 <NA>  <NA>
## 6          6 <NA>     14     9 33101 FL
## 7          7 George   NA     9 <NA>  <NA>
## 8          8 Helen    15     9 90001 CA
```

This fills in missing state information based on ZIP codes without dropping any rows.

Wrap-Up

This lab demonstrated how to identify missing data. You explored how to detect missing values and learned several strategies for handling them, including omitting incomplete records, using imputation to estimate missing values, applying placeholder or filler values where appropriate, and joining with reference data to fill in the blanks. Each of these techniques helps preserve the integrity of your dataset while minimizing distortion or bias.

Exercises

Completion

Dataset 1: Incomplete Hospital Admissions

This dataset simulates hospital admission records where some patient information is missing or incomplete.

```
R Code
admissions <- tibble::tibble(
  PatientID = 201:208,
  Name = c(
    "J. Adams", "R. Bell", "L. Cruz", "M. Diaz",
    NA, "H. Green", "K. Irwin", "N. Jones"
  ),
  Age = c(72, 65, 70, NA, 74, 68, 71, NA),
  Department = c(
    "Cardiology", "Orthopedics", "Cardiology",
    "Neurology", "Cardiology", NA, "Cardiology", "Neurology"
  ),
  Insurance = c(
    "Private", NA, "Medicare", "Medicare",
    "Private", "Medicaid", NA, "Private"
  )
)
```

1. Use colSums(is.na(admissions)) to count the number of missing values in each column.

2. Use summary(admissions) to view basic stats and detect which fields are most often incomplete.

3. Create a new dataset with only complete cases using drop_na(). How many rows remain?

4. Use mutate() and if_else() to impute missing Age as 70 for patients in "Cardiology".

5. How many rows still contain NA in the Age column after imputation?

6. Replace missing values in Insurance with "Unknown". Why might this be risky in real-world analysis?

7. How would you flag any rows where both Age and Insurance were missing?

Dataset 2: Missing Shipment Data

This dataset represents shipping data where some ZIP codes are missing and package weights are partially unreported.

```
R Code
shipments <- tibble::tibble(
  OrderID = 1001:1008,
  ZIP = c(
    "11215", "10001", NA, "60614", NA,
    "33109", "11215", "10001"
  ),
  Weight_kg = c(
    2.5, NA, 3.0, 4.2, NA, 1.8,
    2.5, NA
  )
)
```

8. Use summary() to identify patterns in missing ZIP or Weight_kg values.

9. Replace missing Weight_kg with the average of available weights using mean(..., na.rm = TRUE).

10. Replace missing ZIP codes with "00000" for now. Why might this cause issues when visualizing delivery areas?

11. Suppose you suspect ZIP codes are tied to shipment regions. What kind of reference data could help complete these missing ZIPs more reliably?

12. Use mutate() to flag rows where Weight_kg is imputed. Use a new column WeightFlag with values "Imputed" or "Original".

13. After cleaning, how many total rows contain any NA values?

Lab 12

Relevance

In data analysis, focusing on relevant data is essential to produce meaningful and trustworthy results. Relevant data is timely, meaningful, accurate, and focused on your analysis goals. Removing irrelevant, outdated, or junk data reduces noise and improves clarity. This lab guides you through identifying and retaining only valuable data using R.

Lesson Steps

Step 1: Create Example Dataset with Irrelevant Data

We start with a dataset containing extra spaces, junk values, irrelevant columns, and outdated records.

R Code

```
# Install if not already installed

options(repos = c(CRAN = "https://cran.r-project.org"))
install.packages('tidyverse')
library(tidyverse)
```

R Code

```
students_raw <- tibble::tibble(
  ID = 1:6,
  Name = c(
    " Alice ", "Bob", "Carlos", "Dana",
    "Eva", "Fred"
  ),
  Age = c(15, 14, 15, 14, 14, 13),
  Grade = c(9, 9, 9, 9, 9, 8),
  LastLogin = c(
    "2019-05-01", "2020-11-20", NA, "2024-06-01",
    "2018-03-12", "2023-12-10"
  ),
  SurveyComment = c(
    "Good", "OK", "N/A", "",
    "asdfasd", "xxx"
  ),
  ExtraField1 = c("junk", "junk", "junk", "junk", "
                  junk", "junk")
)

students_raw[, 1:4]
```

Output

```
## # A tibble: 6 x 4
##       ID Name          Age Grade
##    <int> <chr>       <dbl> <dbl>
## 1     1 " Alice "      15     9
## 2     2 "Bob"          14     9
## 3     3 "Carlos"       15     9
## 4     4 "Dana"         14     9
## 5     5 "Eva"          14     9
## 6     6 "Fred"         13     8
```

R Code

```
students_raw[, 5:7]
```

Output

```
## # A tibble: 6 x 3
##    LastLogin   SurveyComment ExtraField1
##    <chr>       <chr>         <chr>
## 1 2019-05-01 "Good"         "junk"
## 2 2020-11-20 "OK"           "junk"
## 3 <NA>        "N/A"          "junk"
## 4 2024-06-01 ""             "junk"
## 5 2018-03-12 "asdfasd"      "\n               junk"
## 6 2023-12-10 "xxx"          "junk"
```

Step 2: Trim Extra Spaces and Remove Junk Values

Remove leading/trailing spaces from text fields and replace meaningless or placeholder values with NA. This flags invalid entries and cleans the data for further processing.

```
R Code
library(dplyr)
library(stringr)

students_clean <- mutate(
  students_raw,
  Name = str_trim(Name),
  SurveyComment = na_if(SurveyComment, "N/A"),
  SurveyComment = na_if(SurveyComment, ""),
  SurveyComment = if_else(SurveyComment == "asdfasd",
    NA_character_, SurveyComment
  )
)

students_clean[, 1:5]
```

Output

```
## # A tibble: 6 x 5
##       ID Name     Age Grade LastLogin
##    <int> <chr>  <dbl> <dbl> <chr>
## 1      1 Alice     15     9 2019-05-01
## 2      2 Bob       14     9 2020-11-20
## 3      3 Carlos    15     9 <NA>
## 4      4 Dana      14     9 2024-06-01
## 5      5 Eva       14     9 2018-03-12
## 6      6 Fred      13     8 2023-12-10
```

R Code

```
students_clean[, 6:7]
```

Output

```
## # A tibble: 6 x 2
##    SurveyComment ExtraField1
##    <chr>         <chr>
## 1 Good          "junk"
## 2 OK            "junk"
## 3 <NA>          "junk"
## 4 <NA>          "junk"
## 5 <NA>          "\n                    junk"
## 6 xxx           "junk"
```

Step 3: Remove Entirely Irrelevant Fields

Drop columns that do not contribute to your analysis goals to keep the dataset focused.

R Code
```
students_clean <- select(students_clean, -ExtraField1)
students_clean[,1:4]
```

Output
```
## # A tibble: 6 x 4
##       ID Name     Age Grade
##    <int> <chr>  <dbl> <dbl>
## 1     1 Alice     15     9
## 2     2 Bob       14     9
## 3     3 Carlos    15     9
## 4     4 Dana      14     9
## 5     5 Eva       14     9
## 6     6 Fred      13     8
```

R Code
```
students_clean[,5:6]
```

Output
```
## # A tibble: 6 x 2
##    LastLogin   SurveyComment
##    <chr>       <chr>
## 1 2019-05-01  Good
## 2 2020-11-20  OK
## 3 <NA>        <NA>
## 4 2024-06-01  <NA>
## 5 2018-03-12  <NA>
## 6 2023-12-10  xxx
```

Step 4: Flag or Filter Outdated Records

Convert date strings to proper Date format and filter out records older than a certain cutoff (e.g., before 2022). This keeps only current and relevant data.

R Code
```
students_clean <- mutate(students_clean,
  LastLogin = as.Date(LastLogin)
)
students_clean <- filter(
  students_clean,
  is.na(LastLogin) | LastLogin >= as.Date("2022-01-01")
)
students_clean
```

Output

```
## # A tibble: 3 x 6
##       ID Name      Age Grade LastLogin   SurveyComment
##    <int> <chr>   <dbl> <dbl> <date>      <chr>
## 1      3 Carlos     15     9 NA          <NA>
## 2      4 Dana       14     9 2024-06-01  <NA>
## 3      6 Fred       13     8 2023-12-10  xxx
```

Step 5: Extract Only Relevant Fields for Analysis

Select only the key variables needed for your specific analysis to simplify and speed up your work.

R Code

```
students_analysis <- select(students_clean, Name, Age, Grade)
students_analysis
```

Output

```
## # A tibble: 3 x 3
##   Name      Age Grade
##   <chr>   <dbl> <dbl>
## 1 Carlos     15     9
## 2 Dana       14     9
## 3 Fred       13     8
```

Wrap-Up

This lab demonstrated practical techniques for identifying and cleaning irrelevant data to improve the quality and focus of your dataset. You worked on trimming extra spaces, removing junk values that add noise, dropping fields that serve no analytic purpose, and filtering out outdated or irrelevant records. You also learned to focus on the columns that matter most for your analysis. Together, these steps help streamline your data, reduce clutter, and ensure that your dataset is accurate, efficient, and ready for meaningful insights.

Exercises

Relevance

Dataset 1: Library Book Checkouts

This dataset represents a set of library records, with junk values, outdated checkouts, and irrelevant metadata.

```
R Code
library_records <- tibble::tibble(
  RecordID = 1:8,
  PatronName = c(
    "  Mia", "Liam ", "Ava", "Noah", "Sophia",
    "N/A", "Lucas", "Emma"
  ),
  BookTitle = c(
    "History of Art", "Science 101", "", "N/A",
    "asdf", "Modern Math", "Biology", "Literature"
  ),
  LastCheckout = c(
    "2017-01-01", "2021-12-31", "2024-01-15",
    "2018-05-20", "2022-10-10", "2024-04-01",
    NA, "2023-03-22"
  ),
  OverdueNotes = c(
    "None", "?", "!!", "", "Lost",
    "NA", "Damaged", "Missing"
  ),
  InternalTag = rep("oldsystem", 8)
)
```

1. Trim extra spaces in the PatronName column using str_trim(). How many names had spacing issues?

2. Use na_if() and if_else() to replace invalid BookTitle values like " "," N/A", or "asdf" with NA. How many titles are now missing?

3. Drop the InternalTag column entirely. Why is it irrelevant for current analysis?

4. Convert LastCheckout to a Date object and filter out rows before January 1, 2022.

5. How many rows remain after filtering outdated records?

6. Replace values in OverdueNotes like "?", "!!", "NA" or " " with NA. Why is this helpful?

7. Select only the fields PatronName, BookTitle, and LastCheckout for analysis. Why might this be a cleaner dataset?

Dataset 2: Survey on Commuting

This survey dataset includes columns with irrelevant text, invalid responses, and outdated records.

R Code

```
commute_survey <- tibble::tibble(
  EntryID = 101:108,
  Respondent = c(
    "Alex", "Taylor", "Jordan", "Riley",
    "Casey", "Jamie", "Morgan", "Quinn"
  ),
  Mode = c(
    "Car", "Bus", "Bike", "N/A", "", "Subway",
    "skateboard", "Bike"
  ),
  Minutes = c(25, 40, 15, 30, 999, NA, 20, 10),
  SubmissionDate = c(
    "2021-12-01", "2022-02-15",
    "2024-01-01", "2023-10-05",
    "2019-08-22", "2022-11-11",
    "2024-05-05", NA
  ),
  ExtraText = rep("remove this", 8)
)
```

8. Use na_if() to replace "N/A" and "" in Mode with NA. Then replace "skateboard" with NA as an invalid mode. How many NA entries are there in Mode?

9. Drop the ExtraText column. Why is it considered irrelevant noise?

10. Replace values of Minutes equal to 999 with NA, assuming this is a placeholder for a missing or corrupted entry.

11. Filter out survey rows submitted before January 1, 2022. How many recent responses remain?

12. Select only the fields Respondent, Mode, Minutes, and SubmissionDate for final analysis.

13. Based on cleaned data, how many valid survey responses include both a commuting mode and time?

Lab 13

Reassigning Data Types

Data types define how R stores and interprets your data. Using incorrect types can cause errors or misleading results in your analysis. For example, ZIP codes stored as numbers lose leading zeros, weights stored as text with units can't be used for calculations, and dates stored as strings can't be manipulated as dates. This lab walks you through identifying and fixing these common problems.

Lesson Steps

Step 1: Load a Sample Dataset with Data Type Problems

To practice, we create a small dataset that simulates typical type issues: ZIP codes as numeric, weights with text units, and birthdates as strings.

R Code
```
# Install if not already installed

options(repos = c(CRAN = "https://cran.r-project.org"))
install.packages("tidyverse")  # run once if needed
library(tidyverse)
```

R Code
```
bad_data <- tibble::tibble(
  Name = c("Alice", "Bob", "Carlos"),
  ZIP = c(2139, 45002, 789),
  Weight = c("130 lbs", "150 lbs", "120 lbs"),
  Birthdate = c("2005-03-15", "2004-07-22", "2006-11-30"),
  Gender = c("Female", "Male", "Female")
)

bad_data
```

Output
```
## # A tibble: 3 x 5
##    Name      ZIP Weight  Birthdate   Gender
##    <chr>   <dbl> <chr>   <chr>       <chr>
## 1 Alice    2139 130 lbs 2005-03-15 Female
## 2 Bob     45002 150 lbs 2004-07-22 Male
## 3 Carlos   789 120 lbs 2006-11-30 Female
```

This dataset will allow us to practice fixing data types and cleaning text fields.

Step 2: Check Current Data Types

Before fixing types, inspect the structure of your dataset to identify which columns have issues. Function glimpse() provides a concise summary showing column types and some sample data.

```
R Code
glimpse(bad_data)
```

```
Output
## Rows: 3
## Columns: 5
## $ Name      <chr> "Alice", "Bob", "Carlos"
## $ ZIP       <dbl> 2139, 45002, 789
## $ Weight    <chr> "130 lbs", "150 lbs", "120 lbs"
## $ Birthdate <chr> "2005-03-15", "2004-07-22", "2006-11-30"
## $ Gender    <chr> "Female", "Male", "Female"
```

This shows ZIP as numeric (which risks losing formatting), Weight as character because of "lbs", and Birthdate as character strings. Identifying these helps us plan the fixes.

Step 3: Fix ZIP Codes

ZIP codes are identifiers, not numbers for calculation. Storing them as numbers can strip leading zeros, causing errors in matching or mapping. We convert ZIP to a character string and pad with leading zeros to standardize 5 digit ZIP formatting. Package stringr can help here.

R Code
```
# Install if not already installed


options(repos = c(CRAN = "https://cran.r-project.org"))
install.packages('stringr')
library(stringr)
```

R Code
```
# Fix zip code data


bad_data$ZIP <- str_pad(as.character(bad_data$ZIP),
                        width = 5, side = "left", pad = "0")


bad_data
```

Output
```
## # A tibble: 3 x 5
##    Name    ZIP   Weight  Birthdate   Gender
##    <chr>   <chr> <chr>   <chr>       <chr>
## 1 Alice   02139 130 lbs 2005-03-15 Female
## 2 Bob     45002 150 lbs 2004-07-22 Male
## 3 Carlos  00789 120 lbs 2006-11-30 Female
```

Now ZIP codes like 2139 become "02139", preserving proper formatting and allowing accurate matching or display.

Step 4: Clean and Convert Weights to Numeric

Weight data here includes the text "lbs", preventing numeric operations. We extract the digits and convert the result to numeric, making the data ready for calculations such as averages or comparisons.

```
R Code
bad_data$Weight_clean <- str_extract(bad_data$Weight, "\\d+")
bad_data$Weight_clean <- as.numeric(bad_data$Weight_clean)


bad_data
```

```
Output
## # A tibble: 3 x 6
##    Name    ZIP    Weight   Birthdate    Gender  Weight_clean
##    <chr>   <chr>  <chr>    <chr>        <chr>          <dbl>
## 1 Alice   02139  130 lbs  2005-03-15   Female           130
## 2 Bob     45002  150 lbs  2004-07-22   Male             150
## 3 Carlos  00789  120 lbs  2006-11-30   Female           120
```

You now have a clean numeric column Weight_clean usable in analysis without being text data.

Step 5: Convert Birthdate to Date Format

Dates stored as character strings cannot be used for date calculations like age or time intervals. Using the lubridate package (part of tidyverse and should have been installed in earlier steps), we convert the Birthdate column to a proper Date object.

R Code
```
library(lubridate)


bad_data$Birthdate <- ymd(bad_data$Birthdate)


glimpse(bad_data)
```

Output
```
## Rows: 3
## Columns: 6
## $ Name         <chr> "Alice", "Bob", "Carlos"
## $ ZIP          <chr> "02139", "45002", "00789"
## $ Weight       <chr> "130 lbs", "150 lbs", "120 lbs"
## $ Birthdate    <date> 2005-03-15, 2004-07-22, 2006-11-30
## $ Gender       <chr> "Female", "Male", "Female"
## $ Weight_clean <dbl> 130, 150, 120
```

With this, you can perform date based operations, such as filtering by age or calculating time spans.

Step 6: Encode Categorical Data

Many analyses or models require categorical data to be encoded numerically. We create a new binary variable Gender_male with 1 for Male and 0 otherwise, preparing it for use in statistical models or machine learning.

R Code

```
bad_data$Gender_male <- if_else(bad_data$Gender == "Male",
   1, 0
)


glimpse(bad_data)
```

Output

```
## Rows: 3
## Columns: 7
## $ Name         <chr> "Alice", "Bob", "Carlos"
## $ ZIP          <chr> "02139", "45002", "00789"
## $ Weight       <chr> "130 lbs", "150 lbs", "120 lbs"
## $ Birthdate    <date> 2005-03-15, 2004-07-22, 2006-11-30
## $ Gender       <chr> "Female", "Male", "Female"
## $ Weight_clean <dbl> 130, 150, 120
## $ Gender_male  <dbl> 0, 1, 0
```

This encoding allows easy inclusion of gender as a predictor in models that require numeric input.

Wrap-Up

This lab showed how to detect and fix common data type issues that can disrupt your analysis. You learned how to properly store ZIP codes as padded character strings, extract numeric values from weight fields, convert string dates into usable Date objects, and encode categorical variables for modeling. Reassigning data types is a key data cleaning step that ensures your data is both accurate and analysis-ready, reducing the risk of silent errors and improving the reliability of your results.

Exercises

Reassigning Data Types

Real-world datasets often contain data stored in the wrong format, such as numbers saved as characters or dates saved as strings. These incorrect data types can lead to problems in calculations, summaries, or visualizations. This lab provides hands-on practice in inspecting and fixing data types using tidyverse, stringr, and lubridate in R.

Dataset 1: Student Info Dataset

```
R Code
library(tidyverse)
library(stringr)
library(lubridate)

student_data <- tibble(
  ID = c(101, 102, 103),
  State = c(94121, 60614, 70119),
  GPA = c("3.8/4", "3.5/4", "3.9/4"),
  DOB = c("07/10/2003", "05/25/2002", "11/03/2004"),
  Status = c("Full Time", "Part Time", "Full Time")
)
```

1. Use glimpse() to check the data types of each column. Which ones appear incorrect for analysis?

2. Convert the State column to character and pad it with leading zeros so it always has 5 characters.

3. Clean the GPA column to remove /4 and convert it to numeric.

4. Convert the DOB column to a proper Date object using lubridate::mdy().

5. Encode the Status column as binary: 1 if "Full Time", 0 otherwise. Add this as a new column.

Dataset 2: Employee Salary Dataset

```
R Code
employee_data <- tibble(
  EmpID = c("A001", "A002", "A003"),
  DeptCode = c(5, 12, 3),
  StartDate = c(
    "2019-01-15", "March 10, 2020",
    "2021/07/01"
  ),
  Salary = c("$55,000", "$63,500", "$47,000"),
  Remote = c("Yes", "No", "Yes")
)
```

6. Use glimpse() to inspect the structure of this dataset. Which columns are not in usable formats?

7. Convert DeptCode to a character column and pad it to always have 3 digits (e.g., "005").

8. Remove currency symbols and commas from the Salary column and convert it to numeric.

9. Convert the StartDate column to a proper date format that R can understand.

10. Create a binary variable Remote_worker where "Yes" = 1 and "No" = 0.

Dataset 3: Product Info Dataset

```r
R Code
product_data <- tibble(
  ProductID = c("P1", "P2", "P3"),
  Release = c("2018", "2019", "2020"),
  Price = c(
    "USD 12.99", "USD 15.50",
    "USD 10.25"
  ),
  Category = c(
    "Electronics", "Books",
    "Electronics"
  ),
  InStock = c("TRUE", "FALSE", "TRUE")
)
```

11. Use glimpse() to identify the column types. What might need converting?

12. Convert Release to numeric.

13. Remove "USD" from the Price column and convert it to numeric.

14. Encode the Category column: 1 for "Electronics", 0 for other categories.

15. Convert the InStock column to a logical (boolean) type using as.logical().

Lab 14

Date and Time Data

Date and time data can be tricky because they often come in different formats, contain missing values, or have unclear time zones. This can make analyzing or comparing dates difficult. In this lab, you will learn how to clean, convert, and work with date-time values in.

Lesson Steps

Step 1: Load Example Data

First, create a small dataset with inconsistent and messy date entries. This example simulates common real-world issues, like different date formats and embedded time zones.

R Code

```
# Install if not already installed

options(repos = c(CRAN = "https://cran.r-project.org"))

# Install packages (run only once)
install.packages("tidyverse")
install.packages("lubridate")

# Load libraries
library(tidyverse)
library(lubridate)
```

R Code
```r
# Simulated messy date-time data

messy_dates <- tibble(
  Name = c("Alice", "Bob", "Carlos", "Dana"),
  Start = c(
    "03/15/2022", "15-Mar-2022",
    "2022.03.15", "March 15, 2022"
  ),
  End = c(
    "03/20/2022", "20-Mar-2022",
    "2022.03.20", "March 20, 2022"
  ),
  Login_Time = c(
    "2022-03-15 08:30",
    "2022-03-15 11:30", "2022-03-15 08:30 PST",
    "2022-03-15 08:30 EST"
  )
)

messy_dates
```

Output
```
## # A tibble: 4 x 4
##    Name   Start          End            Login_Time
##    <chr>  <chr>          <chr>          <chr>
## 1 Alice  03/15/2022     03/20/2022     2022-03-15 08:30
## 2 Bob    15-Mar-2022    20-Mar-2022    2022-03-15 11:30
## 3 Carlos 2022.03.15     2022.03.20     2022-03-15 08:30 PST
## 4 Dana   March 15, 2022 March 20, 2022 2022-03-15 08:30 EST
```

This dataset contains dates in multiple formats and times with different time zones.

Step 2: Convert Text to Date Format

Handling date formats manually can be complex and error-prone. The lubridate package simplifies this with functions that recognize common date formats and convert them to Date objects automatically.

Here, we convert the Start and End columns to proper Date objects so you can perform calculations and comparisons.

R Code
```
messy_dates$Start <- parse_date_time(messy_dates$Start,
   orders = c("mdy", "dmy", "ymd", "B d, Y")
)


messy_dates$End <- parse_date_time(messy_dates$End,
   orders = c("mdy", "dmy", "ymd", "B d, Y")
)
messy_dates[,1:3]
```

Output
```
## # A tibble: 4 x 3
##    Name    Start               End
##    <chr>   <dttm>              <dttm>
## 1 Alice   2022-03-15 00:00:00 2022-03-20 00:00:00
## 2 Bob     2022-03-15 00:00:00 2022-03-20 00:00:00
## 3 Carlos  2022-03-15 00:00:00 2022-03-20 00:00:00
## 4 Dana    2022-03-15 00:00:00 2022-03-20 00:00:00
```

R Code
```
messy_dates[,4]
```

Output
```
## # A tibble: 4 x 1
##    Login_Time
##    <chr>
## 1 2022-03-15 08:30
## 2 2022-03-15 11:30
## 3 2022-03-15 08:30 PST
## 4 2022-03-15 08:30 EST
```

Now, the Start and End columns are standardized Date objects, ready for analysis.

Step 3: Calculate Duration Between Dates

Once dates are properly formatted, you can subtract one date from another to find the time difference. This is useful for measuring duration like task lengths or gaps between events.

R Code
```
# Calculate the number of days btw End and Start
messy_dates$Duration_days <- as.numeric(
  messy_dates$End - messy_dates$Start)


messy_dates[,1:3]
```

Output
```
## # A tibble: 4 x 3
##   Name    Start               End
##   <chr>   <dttm>              <dttm>
## 1 Alice   2022-03-15 00:00:00 2022-03-20 00:00:00
## 2 Bob     2022-03-15 00:00:00 2022-03-20 00:00:00
## 3 Carlos  2022-03-15 00:00:00 2022-03-20 00:00:00
## 4 Dana    2022-03-15 00:00:00 2022-03-20 00:00:00
```

R Code
```
messy_dates[,4:5]
```

Output
```
## # A tibble: 4 x 2
##    Login_Time           Duration_days
##    <chr>                        <dbl>
## 1 2022-03-15 08:30                 5
## 2 2022-03-15 11:30                 5
## 3 2022-03-15 08:30 PST             5
## 4 2022-03-15 08:30 EST             5
```

The new Duration_days column shows the difference in days between the two dates.

Step 4: Add or Subtract Days

You can add or subtract days from a date easily using lubridate. This is helpful for scheduling follow-ups or deadlines based on a start date.

For example, add 5 days to each Start date to create a Followup date:

R Code
```
messy_dates$Followup <- messy_dates$Start + days(5)

messy_dates[,1:3]
```

Output

```
## # A tibble: 4 x 3
##   Name   Start               End
##   <chr>  <dttm>              <dttm>
## 1 Alice  2022-03-15 00:00:00 2022-03-20 00:00:00
## 2 Bob    2022-03-15 00:00:00 2022-03-20 00:00:00
## 3 Carlos 2022-03-15 00:00:00 2022-03-20 00:00:00
## 4 Dana   2022-03-15 00:00:00 2022-03-20 00:00:00
```

R Code

```
messy_dates[,4:6]
```

Output

```
## # A tibble: 4 x 3
##   Login_Time            Duration_days Followup
##   <chr>                         <dbl> <dttm>
## 1 2022-03-15 08:30                  5 2022-03-20 00:00:00
## 2 2022-03-15 11:30                  5 2022-03-20 00:00:00
## 3 2022-03-15 08:30 PST             5 2022-03-20 00:00:00
## 4 2022-03-15 08:30 EST             5 2022-03-20 00:00:00
```

The Followup column now contains dates five days after each start date.

Step 5: Extract Month or Year

Extracting components like the year or month from a date lets you group or summarize data by time periods. This helps with spotting trends or creating time-based visualizations.

184

Create new columns for the year and the month (with month labels):

R Code
```
messy_dates$Start_Year <- year(messy_dates$Start)
messy_dates$Start_Month <- month(messy_dates$Start,
                                  label = TRUE)


messy_dates[,1:3]
```

Output
```
## # A tibble: 4 x 3
##    Name    Start               End
##    <chr>   <dttm>              <dttm>
## 1 Alice   2022-03-15 00:00:00 2022-03-20 00:00:00
## 2 Bob     2022-03-15 00:00:00 2022-03-20 00:00:00
## 3 Carlos  2022-03-15 00:00:00 2022-03-20 00:00:00
## 4 Dana    2022-03-15 00:00:00 2022-03-20 00:00:00
```

R Code
```
messy_dates[,4:5]
```

Output

```
## # A tibble: 4 x 2
##    Login_Time            Duration_days
##    <chr>                         <dbl>
## 1 2022-03-15 08:30                  5
## 2 2022-03-15 11:30                  5
## 3 2022-03-15 08:30 PST              5
## 4 2022-03-15 08:30 EST              5
```

R Code

```
messy_dates[,6:8]
```

Output

```
## # A tibble: 4 x 3
##    Followup              Start_Year Start_Month
##    <dttm>                     <dbl> <ord>
## 1 2022-03-20 00:00:00         2022 Mar
## 2 2022-03-20 00:00:00         2022 Mar
## 3 2022-03-20 00:00:00         2022 Mar
## 4 2022-03-20 00:00:00         2022 Mar
```

Now you can easily group or filter data by month or year for summaries or charts.

Step 6: Convert Text Time to POSIX Date-Time with Time Zones

Working with timestamps including time and time zones requires careful parsing to maintain accuracy across regions. POSIX date-time objects store full date and time info with time zone awareness.

Use lubridate to parse the Login_Time column (which has mixed formats and zones) into standardized POSIX objects and convert them to UTC and Eastern time:

```
R Code
messy_dates$Login_Time_Parsed <- parse_date_time(
  messy_dates$Login_Time,
  orders = c("ymd HM", "ymd HM z"),
  tz = "UTC"
)

messy_dates$Login_Time_UTC <- with_tz(
  messy_dates$Login_Time_Parsed,
  tzone = "UTC"
)
messy_dates$Login_Time_EST <- with_tz(
  messy_dates$Login_Time_Parsed,
  tzone = "America/New_York"
)

messy_dates[,1:3]
```

Output
```
## # A tibble: 4 x 3
##   Name    Start               End
##   <chr>   <dttm>              <dttm>
## 1 Alice   2022-03-15 00:00:00 2022-03-20 00:00:00
## 2 Bob     2022-03-15 00:00:00 2022-03-20 00:00:00
## 3 Carlos  2022-03-15 00:00:00 2022-03-20 00:00:00
## 4 Dana    2022-03-15 00:00:00 2022-03-20 00:00:00
```

R Code
```
messy_dates[,4:5]
```

Output
```
## # A tibble: 4 x 2
##   Login_Time          Duration_days
##   <chr>                        <dbl>
## 1 2022-03-15 08:30                 5
## 2 2022-03-15 11:30                 5
## 3 2022-03-15 08:30 PST             5
## 4 2022-03-15 08:30 EST             5
```

R Code
```
messy_dates[,6:8]
```

Output

```
## # A tibble: 4 x 3
##    Followup            Start_Year Start_Month
##    <dttm>                   <dbl> <ord>
## 1 2022-03-20 00:00:00       2022 Mar
## 2 2022-03-20 00:00:00       2022 Mar
## 3 2022-03-20 00:00:00       2022 Mar
## 4 2022-03-20 00:00:00       2022 Mar
```

R Code

```
messy_dates[,9:10]
```

Output

```
## # A tibble: 4 x 2
##    Login_Time_Parsed   Login_Time_UTC
##    <dttm>              <dttm>
## 1 2022-03-15 08:30:00 2022-03-15 08:30:00
## 2 2022-03-15 11:30:00 2022-03-15 11:30:00
## 3 2022-03-15 08:30:00 2022-03-15 08:30:00
## 4 2022-03-15 08:30:00 2022-03-15 08:30:00
```

R Code

```
messy_dates[,11]
```

Output

```
## # A tibble: 4 x 1
##   Login_Time_EST
##   <dttm>
## 1 2022-03-15 04:30:00
## 2 2022-03-15 07:30:00
## 3 2022-03-15 04:30:00
## 4 2022-03-15 04:30:00
```

This code ensures your timestamps are consistent and comparable, no matter their original time zone.

Wrap-Up

This lab showed how to work with date and time data in a clean, structured way using R. You learned how to convert messy and inconsistent date formats into standardized Date and POSIXct objects using the lubridate package. You also calculated duration, added days to dates, extracted useful components like month and year, and handled time zones properly for accurate timestamp comparisons. These skills are essential for managing and analyzing time and date data.

Exercises

Working with Date and Time Data

Date and time values often come in inconsistent formats or include time zones that make comparisons tricky. Cleaning and standardizing date-time data in R using package lubridate ensures that you can calculate durations, extract time-based insights, and work with timestamps accurately. In this lab, you'll practice cleaning, transforming, and analyzing messy date-time information.

Dataset 1: Hospital Admissions Dataset

```
R Code
library(tidyverse)
library(lubridate)

admissions <- tibble(
  Patient = c("Anna", "Ben", "Charlie"),
  Admit_Date = c("1/4/2021", "2021-04-01", "April 1, 2021"),
  Discharge_Date = c("2021/04/05", "05-Apr-2021", "4-5-2021"),
  Last_Checkup = c(
    "2020-12-01 09:30", "2020-12-01 10:00 EST",
    "2020-12-01 09:00 PST"
  )
)
```

1. Use glimpse() to identify the types of each column. Which ones are problematic for date analysis?

2. Convert Admit_Date and Discharge_Date into Date format using parse_date_time() with appropriate input.

3. Create a new column Stay_Length with the number of days between discharge and admission.

4. Add a column Next_Appointment that is 30 days after Discharge_Date.

5. Convert the Last_Checkup column to POSIXct format. Then create two new columns: one showing the time in UTC, and one in Pacific Time.

Dataset 2: Conference Schedule Dataset

R Code
```
schedule <- tibble(
  Session = c(
    "Opening Keynote", "Workshop A",
    "Panel Discussion"
  ),
  Start_Time = c(
    "2023-06-01 09:00", "2023-06-01 11:30 EST",
    "2023-06-01 14:00 UTC"
  ),
  End_Time = c(
    "2023-06-01 10:30", "2023-06-01 13:00 EST",
    "2023-06-01 15:30 UTC"
  )
)
```

6. Use glimpse() to examine the structure of schedule. What type are the Start_Time and End_Time columns?

7. Parse both Start_Time and End_Time using parse_date_time() and convert them to UTC.

8. Create a column Duration_min that shows session length in minutes.

9. Extract the hour from the Start_Time and create a new column called Start_Hour.

10. Reformat the Start_Time column into America/New_York time using with_tz().

Dataset 3: Social Media Engagement Dataset

```
R Code
posts <- tibble(
  Post_ID = c("X1", "X2", "X3"),
  Posted = c(
    "2024/12/25 08:00 UTC",
    "December 26, 2024 10:00",
    "2024-12-27 12:00 GMT"
  ),
  Clicks = c(102, 87, 134)
)
```

11. Use glimpse() to view the structure. Which date column needs formatting?

12. Convert Posted to POSIXct and normalize all to UTC.

13. Extract the weekday from each post (e.g., Monday, Tuesday).

14. Create a column called Weekend that is TRUE if the post was made on Saturday or Sunday.

15. Calculate how many hours have passed between the post and now using difftime() or Sys.time().

Lab 15

Normalizing and Transforming Data

Data often come in different scales and units, which can make direct comparisons or analyses misleading. Normalization, unit transformations, and handling skewed data are key preparation steps. This lab will show you how to apply these techniques in R, including z-score normalization, unit conversion, log transformations, and financial inflation adjustments.

Lesson Steps

Step 1: Load Data

We start with a simple dataset that records a person's height (in inches) and their salary in the year 2000.

R Code
```
library(tidyverse)

df <- tibble(
  Person = c("A", "B", "C", "D", "E"),
  Height_in = c(60, 64, 72, 65, 67),
  Salary_2000 = c(
    30000, 35000, 50000,
    40000, 45000
  )
)

df
```

Output
```
## # A tibble: 5 x 3
##    Person Height_in Salary_2000
##    <chr>     <dbl>      <dbl>
## 1 A            60       30000
## 2 B            64       35000
## 3 C            72       50000
## 4 D            65       40000
## 5 E            67       45000
```

This dataset simulates height in inches and salaries before any transformation.

Step 2: Normalize a Variable Using Z-Scores

Z-score normalization rescales data by subtracting the mean and dividing by the standard deviation. This centers values around zero with a standard deviation of one, making variables comparable across different units or scales.

This is especially important for methods sensitive to scale differences, like clustering or k-nearest neighbors.

R Code
```
Height_mean <- mean(df$Height_in, na.rm = TRUE)
Height_sd <- sd(df$Height_in, na.rm = TRUE)
df$Height_z <- (df$Height_in - Height_mean) / Height_sd


df
```

Output
```
## # A tibble: 5 x 4
##    Person Height_in Salary_2000 Height_z
##    <chr>      <dbl>       <dbl>    <dbl>
## 1 A             60       30000    -1.27
## 2 B             64       35000   -0.364
## 3 C             72       50000     1.46
## 4 D             65       40000   -0.137
## 5 E             67       45000    0.319
```

The new column Height_z contains normalized heights with mean 0 and standard deviation 1.

Step 3: Transform Units (Inches to Centimeters)

Converting units is a common step to standardize measurements, especially when integrating multiple data sources.

Here we convert heights from inches to centimeters by multiplying by 2.54.

R Code
```
df$Height_cm <- df$Height_in * 2.54

df
```

Output
```
## # A tibble: 5 x 5
##    Person Height_in Salary_2000 Height_z Height_cm
##    <chr>      <dbl>       <dbl>    <dbl>     <dbl>
## 1 A             60       30000    -1.27      152.
## 2 B             64       35000   -0.364      163.
## 3 C             72       50000     1.46      183.
## 4 D             65       40000   -0.137      165.
## 5 E             67       45000    0.319      170.
```

The new Height_cm column now contains heights in centimeters.

Step 4: Apply a Log Transformation

Right-skewed data (such as income or salary) often benefit from a log transformation to reduce skewness, stabilize variance, and help meet assumptions of statistical methods.

To visualize this, we simulate a larger dataset with right-skewed salary data and compare histograms before and after log transformation.

R Code

```
set.seed(123)
Salary_2000 <- rlnorm(1000, meanlog = 10, sdlog = 0.8)
dfsim <- data.frame(Salary_2000 = Salary_2000)

par(mfrow = c(1, 2))

hist(dfsim$Salary_2000, breaks = 40, col = "#637D8D",
     main = "Original Salary Distribution",
     xlab = "Salary", ylab = "Frequency")

hist(log(dfsim$Salary_2000), breaks = 40, col = "#EE6C4D",
     main = "Log-Transformed Salary Distribution",
     xlab = "Log(Salary)", ylab = "Frequency")
```

Original Salary Distributig–Transformed Salary Distr

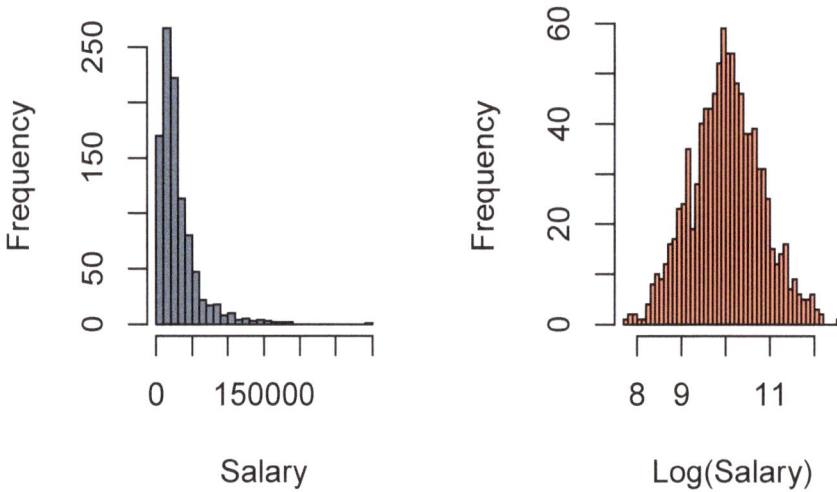

R Code
```
par(mfrow = c(1, 1))
```

The left histogram shows the original skewed distribution, and the right shows how the log transform makes it more symmetric.

Now, apply the log transformation to the smaller sample data:

```
df$Log_Salary <- log(df$Salary_2000)
```

```
df
```

The Log_Salary column contains the natural log of the salary.

Step 5: Adjust Financial Data for Inflation

Financial data collected over many years should be adjusted for inflation to maintain comparability. For example, $50,000 in 2000 has different purchasing power than $50,000 today.

Using a hypothetical inflation multiplier, we adjust the 2000 salaries to 2025 dollars.

R Code
```
# Hypothetical inflation multiplier
adjustment_factor <- 1.7


df$Salary_2025 <- df$Salary_2000 * adjustment_factor


df[,1:4]
```

Output
```
## # A tibble: 5 x 4
##    Person Height_in Salary_2000 Height_z
##    <chr>      <dbl>       <dbl>    <dbl>
## 1 A             60       30000    -1.27
## 2 B             64       35000   -0.364
## 3 C             72       50000     1.46
## 4 D             65       40000   -0.137
## 5 E             67       45000    0.319
```

R Code
```
df[,5:6]
```

Output

```
## # A tibble: 5 x 2
##    Height_cm Salary_2025
##        <dbl>       <dbl>
## 1      152.        51000
## 2      163.        59500
## 3      183.        85000
## 4      165.        68000
## 5      170.        76500
```

The Salary_2025 column reflects inflation-adjusted salaries for better real-world comparison.

Wrap-Up

This lab introduced key techniques for preparing data that vary in scale, units, or distribution. You learned how to normalize variables using z-scores, convert measurements to standard units, apply log transformations to reduce skew, and adjust financial figures for inflation. These steps are essential for making meaningful comparisons, satisfying model assumptions, and ensuring that analyses reflect real-world conditions. By mastering these transformations, you're better equipped to prepare data for statistical modeling, visualization, and interpretation.

Exercises

Normalizing and Transforming Data

Data in real-world scenarios often vary in scale, units, and distribution. To prepare them for analysis, we must normalize features, convert units, and transform skewed distributions. This lab provides practice in z-score normalization, unit conversion, log transformation, and inflation adjustment using real-world inspired data.

Dataset 1: Fitness Metrics

```
R Code
library(tidyverse)

fitness <- tibble(
  Name = c("John", "Leah", "Mike", "Tina", "Sara"),
  Weight_lb = c(180, 145, 200, 135, 150),
  Steps_per_day = c(8000, 9500, 7000, 10000, 8700)
)
```

1. Use glimpse() or str() to identify the current data types. What columns might need transformation?

2. Normalize the Steps_per_day column using z-scores. What are the mean and standard deviation used?

3. Convert Weight_lb to kilograms. (1 lb = 0.453592 kg). Add a new column Weight_kg.

4. Apply a log transformation to the Steps_per_day column and store it as Log_Steps.

5. Explain briefly what the log transformation does to the shape of a right-skewed distribution and when it's appropriate to use.

Dataset 2: Annual Salaries (2010)

```
R Code
salaries <- tibble(
  Employee = c("Alice", "Brian", "Chloe", "Derek", "Ella"),
  Salary_2010 = c(40000, 55000, 60000, 48000, 52000)
)
```

6. Normalize the Salary_2010 column using z-scores. What does a z-score of 0 represent?

7. Add a new column Log_Salary by applying the natural log transformation to Salary_2010.

8. Suppose the inflation multiplier from 2010 to 2025 is 1.45. Create a new column Salary_2025 reflecting the adjusted value.

9. Create a histogram of the original and log-transformed salary data using ggplot2. Describe the difference in distribution.

10. Why is it important to adjust for inflation when comparing salary data over time?

Dataset 3: Car Performance

R Code

```
cars <- tibble(
  Model = c("A", "B", "C", "D", "E"),
  Horsepower = c(150, 180, 130, 220, 160),
  MPG = c(25, 20, 30, 18, 27)
)
```

11. Normalize the Horsepower column using z-scores. Which car is the furthest above the average horsepower?

12. Convert MPG (miles per gallon) to L/100km using the formula: `L_per_100km = 235.215 / MPG`.

13. Apply a log transformation to the Horsepower column and interpret the result.

14. Which variable (MPG or Horsepower) might benefit more from transformation, and why?

15. Create a scatterplot of Log(Horsepower) vs. L_per_100km. Describe any relationship.

Lab 16

Preprocessing Text Data

Text data often contains inconsistencies like irregular capitalization, unwanted symbols, or combined fields that make analysis difficult. Preprocessing text in R lets you clean, structure, and standardize this data, improving accuracy and efficiency for further analysis.

Lesson Steps

Step 1: Load Sample Data

We start by creating a sample dataset with names, state abbreviations, ZIP codes, courses, and some messy text data.

```
R Code
# Install if not already installed

options(repos = c(CRAN = "https://cran.r-project.org"))
install.packages("tidyverse")
library(tidyverse)
```

R Code

```
df <- tibble(
  full_name = c("Smith, John", "Lee, Ann", "Kha, Sue"),
  state = c("ny", "ca", "TX"),
  zip = c("12345", "54321", "78910"),
  course = c("MATH 106", "ENGL 201", "BIOL 110"),
  messy_text = c("Hello! ", "Hi @you", "Test#Case"),
  id = c("001", "002", "003")
)


df
```

Output

```
## # A tibble: 3 x 6
##    full_name    state zip   course   messy_text  id
##    <chr>        <chr> <chr> <chr>    <chr>       <chr>
## 1 Smith, John ny    12345 MATH 106 "Hello! "    001
## 2 Lee, Ann    ca    54321 ENGL 201 "Hi @you"    002
## 3 Kha, Sue    TX    78910 BIOL 110 "Test#Case" 003
```

Step 2: Switch Order of Names (Last, First → First Last)

Names stored as "Last, First" can be inconvenient. We split the full_name column into last and first names, then recombine them into a cleaner "First Last" format.

R Code

```
library(tidyr)


df <- separate(df, col = "full_name",
        into = c("last", "first"), sep = ", ")


df$full_name_clean <- paste(df$first, df$last, sep = " ")


df[,1:5]
```

Output

```
## # A tibble: 3 x 5
##    last  first state zip    course
##    <chr> <chr> <chr> <chr> <chr>
## 1 Smith John  ny     12345 MATH 106
## 2 Lee   Ann   ca     54321 ENGL 201
## 3 Kha   Sue   TX     78910 BIOL 110
```

R Code

```
df[,6:8]
```

Output

```
## # A tibble: 3 x 3
##   messy_text  id    full_name_clean
##   <chr>       <chr> <chr>
## 1 "Hello! "   001   John Smith
## 2 "Hi @you"   002   Ann Lee
## 3 "Test#Case" 003   Sue Kha
```

Step 3: Change Text Case

Standardizing case helps avoid mismatches in text data. Here, we convert the state abbreviations to uppercase.

R Code

```
df$state_upper <- toupper(df$state)

df[,1:5]
```

Output

```
## # A tibble: 3 x 5
##   last  first state zip   course
##   <chr> <chr> <chr> <chr> <chr>
## 1 Smith John  ny    12345 MATH 106
## 2 Lee   Ann   ca    54321 ENGL 201
## 3 Kha   Sue   TX    78910 BIOL 110
```

R Code
```
df[,6:9]
```

Output
```
## # A tibble: 3 x 4
##   messy_text  id    full_name_clean state_upper
##   <chr>       <chr> <chr>           <chr>
## 1 "Hello! "   001   John Smith      NY
## 2 "Hi @you"   002   Ann Lee         CA
## 3 "Test#Case" 003   Sue Kha         TX
```

Step 4: Remove Special Characters and Extra Spaces

Cleaning text by removing unwanted characters and trimming spaces improves data consistency.

R Code
```
# Remove all characters except letters,
# numbers, and spaces from messy_text


df$text_clean <- gsub("[^A-Za-z0-9 ]", "", df$messy_text)


# Remove leading and trailing whitespace


df$text_trimmed <- trimws(df$text_clean)


glimpse(df)
```

```
Output
## Rows: 3
## Columns: 11
## $ last            <chr> "Smith", "Lee", "Kha"
## $ first           <chr> "John", "Ann", "Sue"
## $ state           <chr> "ny", "ca", "TX"
## $ zip             <chr> "12345", "54321", "78910"
## $ course          <chr> "MATH 106", "ENGL 201", "BIOL 110"
## $ messy_text      <chr> "Hello! ", "Hi @you", "Test#Case"
## $ id              <chr> "001", "002", "003"
## $ full_name_clean <chr> "John Smith", "Ann Lee", "Sue Kha"
## $ state_upper     <chr> "NY", "CA", "TX"
## $ text_clean      <chr> "Hello ", "Hi you", "TestCase"
## $ text_trimmed    <chr> "Hello", "Hi you", "TestCase"
```

The text_trimmed column now holds cleaned text ready for analysis.

Step 5: Insert Characters (Format Identifiers)

Formatting codes or IDs by inserting separators improves readability and compatibility. For example, formatting a ZIP+4 code by adding a dash after the fifth digit.

```
R Code
zip_main <- substr(df$zip, 1, 5)
zip_plus4 <- substr(df$zip, 6, 9)
df$zip_formatted <- paste(zip_main, zip_plus4, sep = "-")

glimpse(df)
```

```
Output
## Rows: 3
## Columns: 12
## $ last            <chr> "Smith", "Lee", "Kha"
## $ first           <chr> "John", "Ann", "Sue"
## $ state           <chr> "ny", "ca", "TX"
## $ zip             <chr> "12345", "54321", "78910"
## $ course          <chr> "MATH 106", "ENGL 201", "BIOL 110"
## $ messy_text      <chr> "Hello! ", "Hi @you", "Test#Case"
## $ id              <chr> "001", "002", "003"
## $ full_name_clean <chr> "John Smith", "Ann Lee", "Sue Kha"
## $ state_upper     <chr> "NY", "CA", "TX"
## $ text_clean      <chr> "Hello ", "Hi you", "TestCase"
## $ text_trimmed    <chr> "Hello", "Hi you", "TestCase"
## $ zip_formatted   <chr> "12345-", "54321-", "78910-"
```

The zip_formatted column now contains standardized ZIP codes like "12345-6789".

Step 6: Split Text into Parts (Tokenize)

Tokenization splits combined text fields into components. Here, we split course codes into subject and number.

R Code

```
df <- tidyr::separate(df,
  col = "course",
  into = c("subject", "number"), sep = " "
)


glimpse(df)
```

Output

```
## Rows: 3
## Columns: 13
## $ last            <chr> "Smith", "Lee", "Kha"
## $ first           <chr> "John", "Ann", "Sue"
## $ state           <chr> "ny", "ca", "TX"
## $ zip             <chr> "12345", "54321", "78910"
## $ subject         <chr> "MATH", "ENGL", "BIOL"
## $ number          <chr> "106", "201", "110"
## $ messy_text      <chr> "Hello! ", "Hi @you", "Test#Case"
## $ id              <chr> "001", "002", "003"
## $ full_name_clean <chr> "John Smith", "Ann Lee", "Sue Kha"
## $ state_upper     <chr> "NY", "CA", "TX"
## $ text_clean      <chr> "Hello ", "Hi you", "TestCase"
## $ text_trimmed    <chr> "Hello", "Hi you", "TestCase"
## $ zip_formatted   <chr> "12345-", "54321-", "78910-"
```

Now, subject holds the course prefix (e.g., "MATH") and number holds the course number (e.g., "106").

214

Step 7: Concatenate Text Fields

Combining text fields creates new formatted labels or IDs. We create a formatted course code and add a prefix to IDs.

```
R Code
df$full_course <- paste(df$subject, df$number, sep = "-")


df$id_with_prefix <- paste0("STU_", df$id)


glimpse(df)
```

```
Output
## Rows: 3
## Columns: 15
## $ last            <chr> "Smith", "Lee", "Kha"
## $ first           <chr> "John", "Ann", "Sue"
## $ state           <chr> "ny", "ca", "TX"
## $ zip             <chr> "12345", "54321", "78910"
## $ subject         <chr> "MATH", "ENGL", "BIOL"
## $ number          <chr> "106", "201", "110"
## $ messy_text      <chr> "Hello! ", "Hi @you", "Test#Case"
## $ id              <chr> "001", "002", "003"
## $ full_name_clean <chr> "John Smith", "Ann Lee", "Sue Kha"
## $ state_upper     <chr> "NY", "CA", "TX"
## $ text_clean      <chr> "Hello ", "Hi you", "TestCase"
## $ text_trimmed    <chr> "Hello", "Hi you", "TestCase"
## $ zip_formatted   <chr> "12345-", "54321-", "78910-"
## $ full_course     <chr> "MATH-106", "ENGL-201", "BIOL-110"
## $ id_with_prefix  <chr> "STU_001", "STU_002", "STU_003"
```

The dataset now includes user-friendly, consistent text fields like "MATH-106" and "STU_001".

Wrap-Up

This lab demonstrated essential techniques for preprocessing text data to improve its consistency and usability. You practiced splitting and reordering names, standardizing text case, removing unwanted characters, formatting identifiers, and tokenizing combined fields. Additionally, you learned how to concatenate fields to create clear, standardized labels. These steps help clean messy text data, making it ready for analysis, matching, or reporting.

Exercises

Preprocessing Text Data

Messy text data can contain inconsistent capitalization, special characters, mixed formats, or multiple fields crammed together. Cleaning and structuring text is essential for quality analysis. In this exercise, you'll perform common text preprocessing tasks like splitting names, standardizing case, cleaning characters, formatting identifiers, and tokenizing fields.

Dataset 1: Student Info and Notes

```
R Code
library(tidyverse)

students <- tibble(
  full_name = c("Nguyen, Bao", "Taylor, Mia", "Singh, Ravi"),
  state = c("fl", "NY", "Tx"),
  zip = c("32100", "10027", "77005"),
  note = c("Good! ", "Nice work @Mia", "#LateSubmission "),
  id = c("101", "102", "103"),
  course = c("HIST 101", "CHEM 120", "PSYC 230")
)
```

1. Split the full_name column into last and first, and create a new column full_name_clean in "First Last" format.

2. Convert the state abbreviations to uppercase and save the result as a new column state_upper.

3. Remove all special characters (anything not a letter, number, or space) from the note column. Name the new column note_clean.

4. Trim any extra spaces in note_clean and store the result as note_trimmed. What is the cleaned note text for Ravi?

5. Use string concatenation to create a student_code column in the format "STU-101", "STU-102", etc., using the id.

Dataset 2: Library Catalog

```
R Code
library(tidyverse)

books <- tibble(
  title = c(
    "Intro to R", "Data Science!",
    "Machine_Learning@2025"
  ),
  author = c(
    "Hadley, Wickham", "Grolemund, Garrett",
    "James, Gareth"
  ),
  code = c("R001", "DS101", "ML400"),
  call_number = c("QA76.73", "QA76.9", "QA76.6")
)
```

6. Split the author field into last and first names, and reformat it as First Last in a new column author_clean.

7. Remove any punctuation or special symbols from the title column and save it as title_clean.

8. Extract the course prefix (e.g., "DS") and number (e.g., "101") from the code column into two new columns subject and number.

9. Combine subject and number into a single formatted code (e.g., "DS-101") in a new column formatted_code.

10. Using the call_number column, add a prefix "CALL_" to each number. What is the final result for all three?

Dataset 3: Customer Submissions

```
R Code
library(tibble)

submissions <- tibble(
  name = c(
    "Rodriguez, Elena", "O'Neil, Sam",
    "Chen, Mei"
  ),
  email = c(
    "elena@ex.com", "sam@domain.org",
    "mei@edu.net"
  ),
  feedback = c(
    "Awesome!!", "Late #response",
    "@support not helpful..."
  ),
  ticket = c("0001", "0002", "0003")
)
```

11. Split the name column and reassemble it as First Last in a new column name_clean.

12. Remove special characters from feedback and store the result as feedback_clean.

13. Trim whitespace from the cleaned feedback text. Which user had a trimmed feedback value of "Late response"?

14. Add a prefix "TCK_" to the ticket column to create ticket_id.

15. Combine name_clean and ticket_id into a single summary ID (e.g., "Elena Rodriguez - TCK_0001"). What are the final values?

Lab 17

Binning Data

In data analysis, we often work with variables that have a wide range of values. Sometimes these values are too spread out to interpret easily or use directly in models. Binning is the process of grouping these values into ranges or categories. This makes it easier to spot patterns, reduces noise, and can improve model performance or interpretability. For example, instead of analyzing exact ages, we can group people into categories like "Child" or "Senior."

Lesson Steps

Step 1: Create a vector of continuous data

We start with a simple numeric vector that contains ages. Using a vector keeps this example focused on binning a single variable.

```
R Code
# A sample of age data

ages <- c(5, 12, 17, 24, 32, 45, 52, 63, 78)
```

This vector contains age values we will group into bins.

Step 2: Use `cut()` to bin the data

The cut function is used to divide continuous numeric data into intervals, or bins, based on the breakpoints you provide. The breaks argument defines the edges of each bin, such as from 0 to 12, 13 to 19, and so on. The labels argument assigns a descriptive name to each bin, like "Child" or "Teenager". Setting right to TRUE means the intervals will include the right endpoint, so a value like age 12 would be included in the "Child" group. The include.lowest argument, when set to TRUE, makes sure that the smallest value in the dataset is included in the first bin.

R Code
```
# Define bins and labels

age_bins <- cut(
  ages,
  breaks = c(0, 12, 19, 35, 55, Inf),
  labels = c(
    "Child", "Teenager", "Young Adult",
    "Adult", "Senior"
  ),
  right = TRUE,
  include.lowest = TRUE
)
```

This creates a factor vector where each age is assigned to one of the bins.

Step 3: View the binned data

To see the original ages alongside their assigned bins, we combine them into a data frame.

```
R Code
# View the result


df <- data.frame(Age = ages, Age_Group = age_bins)
df
```

```
Output
##    Age    Age_Group
## 1    5        Child
## 2   12        Child
## 3   17     Teenager
## 4   24 Young Adult
## 5   32 Young Adult
## 6   45        Adult
## 7   52        Adult
## 8   63       Senior
## 9   78       Senior
```

Step 4: Define categorical data

Sometimes categorical data like college majors need to be grouped into broader categories. This simplifies the data, making it easier to analyze and interpret.

```
R Code
# List of specific college majors


majors <- c(
   "Biology", "Nutrition", "Chemistry",
   "Philosophy", "History", "English"
)
```

Step 5: Map categories to broader groups

We create a lookup vector that maps each major to a broader field, such as "Science" or "Humanities." This reduces the number of unique categories.

```
R Code
# Map each major to a broader field using a named vector


field_lookup <- c(
   "Biology" = "Science",
   "Nutrition" = "Science",
   "Chemistry" = "Science",
   "Philosophy" = "Humanities",
   "History" = "Humanities",
   "English" = "Humanities"
)
```

Step 6: Assign categories

Using the lookup vector, we assign each major to its broader field.

R Code
```
# Assign each major to its corresponding field category


fields <- field_lookup[majors]
```

Step 7: View the categorized data

Finally, we combine the majors and their mapped fields into a data frame to view the results.

R Code
```
# Combine into a data frame to view the results


data.frame(Major = majors, Field = fields)
```

Output
```
##                   Major       Field
## Biology         Biology     Science
## Nutrition       Nutrition   Science
## Chemistry       Chemistry   Science
## Philosophy      Philosophy  Humanities
## History           History   Humanities
## English           English   Humanities
```

Wrap-Up

This lab introduced the concept of binning to simplify and organize data for easier analysis. You learned how to group continuous numeric values

into meaningful categories using the cut() function, which helps reveal patterns and reduces complexity. You also saw how to map detailed categorical data into broader groups by creating a lookup table, making categories
easier to interpret and analyze. Binning techniques are valuable preprocessing steps for summarizing and graphing data, improving visualization clarity,
and preparing variables for modeling.

Exercises

The following dataset represents average daily screen time (in hours) for 12 high school students over a two-week period.

```
R Code
screen_hours <- c(
  1.5, 2.2, 5.8, 3.0, 6.5, 7.3,
  4.9, 8.0, 3.5, 2.7, 6.0, 9.1
)
```

Each value shows how many hours a student spends on screens (phone, computer, or TV) per day on average.

1. Use cut() to group the screen time values into these categories: 0 to 2 as "Very Low", 2 to 4 as "Low", 4 to 6 as "Moderate", 6 to 8 as "High", and above 8 as "Very High". What label is assigned to the value 6.5?

2. How many students fall into each screen time group? Use table() to count the frequencies.

3. What percentage of students are in the "High" or "Very High" categories?

4. Which group contains the median screen time value?

5. Create a new data frame that contains both the original screen time and the assigned category.

6. Sort the data frame from highest to lowest screen time. What category does the student with the second-highest screen time belong to?

7. Use cut(..., breaks = 3) to divide the data into three equal-width intervals. What are the numerical breakpoints R uses?

8. How do the equal-width categories compare to the manually defined categories in question 1? Describe one key difference in how students are grouped.

9. Create a bar plot that shows the number of students in each custom screen time category from question 1.

10. What is the screen time value for the student who falls exactly on a bin edge? Explain how cut() assigns values that fall on breakpoints when right = TRUE.

Lab 18

Changing the Type of Data Structure

Data restructuring means changing how a dataset is organized or shaped to better support analysis, modeling, or visualization. Unlike filtering or sorting, restructuring permanently changes the organization of your data. This can involve subsetting, aggregating, joining, or pivoting data. The goal is to prepare the data to fit your specific analytical needs, such as making it compatible with certain software or simplifying it for other users.

Lesson Steps

Step 1: Install and load the tidyverse package

Before working with tibbles, install and load the tidyverse package, which includes useful tools for data science.

```
R Code
# Install if not already installed

options(repos = c(CRAN = "https://cran.r-project.org"))
install.packages("tidyverse")
library(tidyverse)
```

Step 2: Example of why to do this

One common restructuring step in R is converting a basic data frame into a tibble. A tibble is a modern version of a data frame designed to work smoothly within the tidyverse, which is a set of R packages that share a consistent syntax and philosophy. Using tibbles helps make your data workflows more intuitive and less error-prone.

Both data frames and tibbles store tabular data, but tibbles offer an improved user experience in several ways. They display cleaner and easier-to-read output, making it simpler to interpret the data at a glance. Tibbles also handle large datasets more efficiently and consistently preserve variable types—for example, they do not automatically convert character strings into factors. Additionally, when printed, tibbles show only the first few rows and columns, preventing your console from being overwhelmed with too much information. Converting a data frame to a tibble does not alter the underlying data; it simply changes how the data is presented and managed within your workflow.

Step 3: Create a basic data frame

Let's start by creating a simple data frame with names and scores.

```
R Code
# Basic data frame
df <- data.frame(
  Name = c("Alice", "Bob", "Carlos"),
  Score = c(85, 90, 88)
)
```

Step 4: Convert the data frame to a tibble

Use the `as_tibble()` function from the tidyverse to convert the data frame into a tibble.

R Code
```
# Convert to tibble (modern data frame)


tbl <- as_tibble(df)
```

Step 5: View the data frame and tibble

Print both the original data frame and the new tibble to compare their outputs.

R Code
```
# View data frame


df
```

Output
```
##      Name Score
## 1   Alice    85
## 2     Bob    90
## 3 Carlos    88
```

R Code
```
# View tibble


print(tbl)
```

Output
```
## # A tibble: 3 x 2
##    Name    Score
##    <chr>   <dbl>
## 1 Alice      85
## 2 Bob        90
## 3 Carlos     88
```

You will notice that the tibble output is cleaner and easier to read, especially with larger datasets. This small restructuring step helps your analysis run smoother and reduces common data type issues.

Wrap-Up

This lab introduced a basic but important data restructuring step in R: converting a traditional data frame into a tibble. This change doesn't alter the underlying data but improves how it is displayed and interacted with, especially within tidyverse workflows. While this example focused on one R-specific structure change, it reflects a broader category of data restructuring tasks common in analytics. These transformations help make your data easier to manage, visualize, and analyze in a consistent and efficient way.

Exercises

Changing the Type of Data Structure

This lab focuses on changing how data is structured in R by converting standard data frames into tibbles. Tibbles are modern versions of data frames that are easier to read, safer to use, and work better with tidyverse tools. In this exercise you will make simple datasets, convert them into tibbles, and reflect on the differences in structure and output.

Data Set 1: Employee Performance

This dataset contains information about four employees, including their department and performance score.

```
R Code
emp_df <- data.frame(
   Employee = c("John", "Priya", "Ling", "Marco"),
   Department = c("Sales", "IT", "HR", "Marketing"),
   Score = c(92, 88, 75, 80)
)
```

1. Convert emp_df into a tibble and assign it to a new variable called emp_tbl.

2. Print both emp_df and emp_tbl. What differences do you see in how the outputs are displayed in the console?

3. Use the class() function on emp_df and emp_tbl. What are the class types of each object?

4. Use the names() function to show the column names of emp_df and emp_tbl. Are the results the same?

235

5. Add a new column named Bonus to emp_df with values (9.2, 8.8, 7.5, 8.0). Create a new tibble version of the updated data.

Data Set 2: Bookstore Inventory

This dataset lists several books, their price, stock quantity, and whether they are bestsellers.

```
R Code
books_df <- data.frame(
   Title = c("Data Science 101", "R for Everyone", "Tidy Data"),
   Price = c(39.99, 29.95, 45.50),
   Stock = c(12, 5, 8),
   Bestseller = c(TRUE, TRUE, FALSE)
)
```

6. Convert books_df into a tibble called books_tbl.

7. Print both books_df and books_tbl. How does the tibble display differently?

8. Use the dim() function on books_df and books_tbl. What does it return?

9. Use print() with the argument n = 2 to show only the first two rows of books_tbl.

10. Replace the entire Stock column in books_df with new values (10, 4, 6). Print both the updated data frame and its tibble version.

Data Set 3: Fitness Tracker

This dataset contains step counts, calories burned, and minutes active for four users.

R Code
```
fit_df <- data.frame(
  User = c("Anna", "Ben", "Chris", "Dana"),
  Steps = c(9500, 12000, 8700, 10000),
  Calories = c(300, 420, 280, 360),
  Minutes = c(45, 60, 35, 50)
)
```

11. Convert the data frame to a tibble named fit_tbl.

12. Print both fit_df and fit_tbl. Which format is easier to read?

13. What is the result of running class(fit_df) and class(fit_tbl)?

14. Use names() to list the column names in fit_tbl.

15. Write one sentence about why tibbles are useful when working with structured data in R.

Lab 19

Changing Variable Names and Order

Changing variable names and the order of columns is a simple but important step in restructuring data. Many real-world datasets have unclear or generic column names like X1 or data1. These vague names make it hard to understand the data and can lead to mistakes during analysis. Renaming columns to meaningful names improves clarity and helps avoid confusion.

Consistent variable names are especially important when combining data from multiple sources. Matching fields correctly depends on having the same names. Reordering columns also helps by grouping related variables together or putting the most important ones at the start. This makes the dataset easier to read and work with, especially when sharing results or making reports.

It's important to document any renaming or reordering so others (and you) can follow the changes. Update all your scripts and notes to reflect new names or order. Clear documentation prevents errors and misunderstandings.

Now let's practice renaming and reordering variables in R using the built-in mtcars dataset and the dplyr package from tidyverse.

Lesson Steps

Step 1: Load the data and required package

First, load the dplyr package and preview the mtcars dataset.

```
R Code
library(dplyr)

data("mtcars")

# Load dataset
data <- head(mtcars)

# Split into first 6 columns and remaining columns
first_part <- data[, 1:6]
second_part <- data[, 7:ncol(data)]

# Format and print both sections with a separator
cat("=== First 6 Columns ===\n",
    paste(capture.output(print(first_part)),
          collapse = "\n"),
    "\n\n=== Remaining Columns ===\n",
    paste(capture.output(print(second_part)),
          collapse = "\n"),
    sep = "\n")
```

```
Output
## === First 6 Columns ===
##
##                      mpg cyl disp  hp drat    wt
## Mazda RX4           21.0   6  160 110 3.90 2.620
## Mazda RX4 Wag       21.0   6  160 110 3.90 2.875
## Datsun 710          22.8   4  108  93 3.85 2.320
## Hornet 4 Drive      21.4   6  258 110 3.08 3.215
## Hornet Sportabout   18.7   8  360 175 3.15 3.440
## Valiant             18.1   6  225 105 2.76 3.460
##
##
## === Remaining Columns ===
##
##                      qsec vs am gear carb
## Mazda RX4           16.46  0  1    4    4
## Mazda RX4 Wag       17.02  0  1    4    4
## Datsun 710          18.61  1  1    4    1
## Hornet 4 Drive      19.44  1  0    3    1
## Hornet Sportabout   17.02  0  0    3    2
## Valiant             20.22  1  0    3    1
```

This shows the first few rows of the dataset with original variable names.

Step 2: Rename variables

Renaming variables helps make their meaning clear. You can rename one or several columns at once.

R Code

```r
# Rename one column: 'mpg' to 'miles_per_gallon'
mtcars_renamed <- rename(mtcars, miles_per_gallon = mpg)



# Load dataset
data <- head(mtcars_renamed)


# Split into first 6 columns and remaining columns
first_part <- data[, 1:6]
second_part <- data[, 7:ncol(data)]


# Format and print both sections with a separator
cat("=== First 6 Columns ===\n",
    paste(capture.output(print(first_part)),
          collapse = "\n"),
    "\n\n=== Remaining Columns ===\n",
    paste(capture.output(print(second_part)),
          collapse = "\n"),
    sep = "\n")
```

Output

```
## === First 6 Columns ===
##
##                   miles_per_gallon cyl disp  hp drat    wt
## Mazda RX4                     21.0   6  160 110 3.90 2.620
## Mazda RX4 Wag                 21.0   6  160 110 3.90 2.875
## Datsun 710                    22.8   4  108  93 3.85 2.320
## Hornet 4 Drive                21.4   6  258 110 3.08 3.215
## Hornet Sportabout             18.7   8  360 175 3.15 3.440
## Valiant                       18.1   6  225 105 2.76 3.460
##
##
## === Remaining Columns ===
##
##                    qsec vs am gear carb
## Mazda RX4         16.46  0  1    4    4
## Mazda RX4 Wag     17.02  0  1    4    4
## Datsun 710        18.61  1  1    4    1
## Hornet 4 Drive    19.44  1  0    3    1
## Hornet Sportabout 17.02  0  0    3    2
## Valiant           20.22  1  0    3    1
```

This renames the mpg column to miles_per_gallon for clarity.

To rename multiple columns, list them all in the rename() function:

R Code

```
# Rename multiple columns for better clarity


mtcars_renamed <- rename(mtcars,
  miles_per_gallon = mpg,
  horsepower = hp,
  weight = wt
)


# Load dataset
data <- head(mtcars)


# Split into first 6 columns and remaining columns
first_part <- data[, 1:6]
second_part <- data[, 7:ncol(data)]


# Format and print both sections with a separator
cat("=== First 6 Columns ===\n",
    paste(capture.output(print(first_part)),
          collapse = "\n"),
    "\n\n=== Remaining Columns ===\n",
    paste(capture.output(print(second_part)),
          collapse = "\n"),
    sep = "\n")
```

Output

```
## === First 6 Columns ===
##
##                       mpg cyl disp  hp drat    wt
## Mazda RX4            21.0   6  160 110 3.90 2.620
## Mazda RX4 Wag        21.0   6  160 110 3.90 2.875
## Datsun 710           22.8   4  108  93 3.85 2.320
## Hornet 4 Drive       21.4   6  258 110 3.08 3.215
## Hornet Sportabout    18.7   8  360 175 3.15 3.440
## Valiant              18.1   6  225 105 2.76 3.460
##
##
## === Remaining Columns ===
##
##                       qsec vs am gear carb
## Mazda RX4            16.46  0  1    4    4
## Mazda RX4 Wag        17.02  0  1    4    4
## Datsun 710           18.61  1  1    4    1
## Hornet 4 Drive       19.44  1  0    3    1
## Hornet Sportabout    17.02  0  0    3    2
## Valiant              20.22  1  0    3    1
```

Now the dataset has three clearer variable names: `miles_per_gallon`, `horsepower`, and `weight`.

Step 3: Reorder columns

Changing the order of columns helps highlight important variables or groups of variables. Use the `select()` function from `dplyr` to reorder columns easily.

245

R Code

```
# Move 'cyl' and 'hp' columns to the front
# keep all others after


mtcars_reordered <- select(mtcars, cyl, hp, everything())



# Load dataset
data <- head(mtcars_reordered)


# Split into first 6 columns and remaining columns
first_part <- data[, 1:6]
second_part <- data[, 7:ncol(data)]


# Format and print both sections with a separator
cat("=== First 6 Columns ===\n",
    paste(capture.output(print(first_part)),
          collapse = "\n"),
    "\n\n=== Remaining Columns ===\n",
    paste(capture.output(print(second_part)),
          collapse = "\n"),
    sep = "\n")
```

Output

```
## === First 6 Columns ===
##
##                   cyl  hp  mpg disp drat    wt
## Mazda RX4           6 110 21.0  160 3.90 2.620
## Mazda RX4 Wag       6 110 21.0  160 3.90 2.875
## Datsun 710          4  93 22.8  108 3.85 2.320
## Hornet 4 Drive      6 110 21.4  258 3.08 3.215
## Hornet Sportabout   8 175 18.7  360 3.15 3.440
## Valiant             6 105 18.1  225 2.76 3.460
##
##
## === Remaining Columns ===
##
##                  qsec vs am gear carb
## Mazda RX4        16.46  0  1    4    4
## Mazda RX4 Wag    17.02  0  1    4    4
## Datsun 710       18.61  1  1    4    1
## Hornet 4 Drive   19.44  1  0    3    1
## Hornet Sportabout 17.02 0  0    3    2
## Valiant          20.22  1  0    3    1
```

This moves the cyl (cylinders) and hp (horsepower) columns to the start, with the rest following in their original order.

To move a column to the end, remove it and then add it back last:

R Code

```
# Move 'mpg' to the end by excluding it first
# then adding it last
mtcars_moved <- select(mtcars, -mpg, mpg)



# Load dataset
data <- head(mtcars_moved)


# Split into first 6 columns and remaining columns
first_part <- data[, 1:6]
second_part <- data[, 7:ncol(data)]


# Format and print both sections with a separator
cat("=== First 6 Columns ===\n",
    paste(capture.output(print(first_part)),
          collapse = "\n"),
    "\n\n=== Remaining Columns ===\n",
    paste(capture.output(print(second_part)),
          collapse = "\n"),
    sep = "\n")
```

Output

```
## === First 6 Columns ===
##
##                    cyl disp  hp drat    wt  qsec
## Mazda RX4            6  160 110 3.90 2.620 16.46
## Mazda RX4 Wag        6  160 110 3.90 2.875 17.02
## Datsun 710           4  108  93 3.85 2.320 18.61
## Hornet 4 Drive       6  258 110 3.08 3.215 19.44
## Hornet Sportabout    8  360 175 3.15 3.440 17.02
## Valiant              6  225 105 2.76 3.460 20.22
##
##
## === Remaining Columns ===
##
##                    vs am gear carb  mpg
## Mazda RX4           0  1    4    4 21.0
## Mazda RX4 Wag       0  1    4    4 21.0
## Datsun 710          1  1    4    1 22.8
## Hornet 4 Drive      1  0    3    1 21.4
## Hornet Sportabout   0  0    3    2 18.7
## Valiant             1  0    3    1 18.1
```

This effectively puts the mpg column at the end of the dataset.

Wrap-Up

Renaming and reordering variables in R is straightforward but should be done carefully. Clear names reduce confusion and help avoid mistakes in your analysis or when merging data. Always keep track of your changes with comments or notes to make your work reproducible and understandable to others. Avoid duplicate column names, and update all code that uses renamed variables to keep everything consistent.

Exercises

Changing Variable Names and Order

Renaming and reordering columns helps make datasets easier to understand and analyze. This exercise uses simple custom datasets to practice these skills using only `rename()` and `select()` from the `dplyr` package.

Data Set 1: Student Enrollment

This dataset includes information about students, the year they enrolled, and their declared major.

```
R Code
library(dplyr)

enroll_df <- data.frame(
  ID = c(101, 102, 103, 104),
  Yr = c(2021, 2022, 2022, 2023),
  Maj = c("Biology", "Math", "History", "English")
)
```

1. Rename the column Yr to Year.

2. Rename Maj to Major.

3. What are the new column names? Use the names() function to print them.

4. Use select() to move Major to be the first column.

5. Why might someone prefer to have Major appear first in this dataset?

Data Set 2: Small Business Sales

This dataset tracks monthly sales, expenses, and profit for three small businesses.

```
R Code
sales_df <- data.frame(
    Business = c("Apex", "Beacon", "Civic"),
    Jan = c(10000, 8500, 9200),
    Feb = c(12000, 9000, 9700),
    Profit = c(4000, 3000, 3300)
)
```

6. Rename Jan and Feb to January_Sales and February_Sales.

7. Rename Profit to Total_Profit.

8. Use names() to confirm your changes.

9. Reorder the columns so Total_Profit is the second column.

10. What advantage might this new column order have when analyzing sales trends?

Data Set 3: Pet Records

This dataset stores information on pets in a shelter.

R Code

```
pets_df <- data.frame(
   PetID = c(201, 202, 203),
   Breed = c("Labrador", "Tabby", "Poodle"),
   Age = c(3, 2, 5),
   Adopted = c(TRUE, FALSE, TRUE)
)
```

11. Rename PetID to ID_Number.

12. Rename Adopted to `Is_Adopted`.

13. Move Is_Adopted' to the first column.

14. What is now the third column in the dataset?

15. Why is it important to keep column names clear and descriptive in records like this?

Lab 20

Aggregated or Summary Datasets

Aggregation is a key data restructuring technique. It involves summarizing detailed datasets into simpler forms—such as totals, averages, or counts—to help identify patterns and support specific types of analysis. While aggregation often creates a smaller dataset, it doesn't replace the original data. You usually want to keep both versions: the full dataset and the aggregated summaries.

Lesson Steps

Step 1: Create a sample dataset

We'll start by creating a simple dataset that records sales for different products at different store locations.

R Code

```
# Load the dplyr package for data manipulation
library(dplyr)

# Create a sample dataset of store sales
sales_data <- data.frame(
  Store = c("A", "A", "B", "B", "C", "C"),
  Product = c(
    "Apples", "Oranges", "Apples", "Oranges",
    "Apples", "Oranges"
  ),
  Sales = c(100, 150, 120, 130, 90, 160)
)

# View the first few rows
head(sales_data)
```

Output

```
##    Store Product Sales
## 1     A  Apples   100
## 2     A Oranges   150
## 3     B  Apples   120
## 4     B Oranges   130
## 5     C  Apples    90
## 6     C Oranges   160
```

This creates a data frame with store names, product types, and sales amounts.

Step 2: Calculate total sales by store

We can group the data by store and sum the sales for each one.

```
R Code
# Group by Store
grouped_store <- group_by(sales_data, Store)

# Calculate total sales for each store
total_sales_store <- summarise(grouped_store,
  TotalSales = sum(Sales)
)

# View the result
total_sales_store
```

```
Output
## # A tibble: 3 x 2
##    Store TotalSales
##    <chr>      <dbl>
## 1 A            250
## 2 B            250
## 3 C            250
```

This produces a new summary table with the total sales per store.

Step 3: Calculate average sales by product

Now let's group the data by product and compute the average sales for each type.

R Code
```
# Group by Product
grouped_product <- group_by(sales_data, Product)


# Calculate average sales for each product
avg_sales_product <- summarise(grouped_product,
  AvgSales = mean(Sales)
)


# View the result
avg_sales_product
```

Output
```
## # A tibble: 2 x 2
##   Product AvgSales
##   <chr>      <dbl>
## 1 Apples      103.
## 2 Oranges     147.
```

This creates a summary table showing the average sales for apples and oranges.

Step 4: Summarize sales by both store and product

We can also group by multiple variables to get more detailed summaries.

R Code

```r
# Group by both Store and Product
grouped_store_product <- group_by(sales_data, Store, Product)

# Count number of records and calculate average sales
summary_store_product <- summarise(grouped_store_product,
  Count = n(),
  AvgSales = mean(Sales)
)

# View the summary
summary_store_product
```

Output

```
## # A tibble: 6 x 4
## # Groups:   Store [3]
##    Store Product Count AvgSales
##    <chr> <chr>   <int>    <dbl>
## 1 A      Apples     1      100
## 2 A      Oranges    1      150
## 3 B      Apples     1      120
## 4 B      Oranges    1      130
## 5 C      Apples     1       90
## 6 C      Oranges    1      160
```

This shows how many sales records exist for each store-product combination and their average sales.

Wrap-Up

This lab demonstrated how to use grouping and summarization in R to restructure a dataset into aggregated views. We grouped data by one or more variables and applied summary functions to generate totals, averages, and counts. These summary tables are useful for specific analyses, but they should be used alongside the original, more detailed data, not as replacements.

Exercises

Aggregated or Summary Datasets

Aggregation summarizes raw data to make patterns clearer and analysis easier. These exercises give you practice using group_by() and summarise() to compute totals, averages, and counts in simplified datasets.

Data Set 1: Library Checkouts

This dataset records the number of books checked out by patrons at three different libraries.

```
R Code
library(dplyr)

checkout_data <- data.frame(
  Library = c(
    "East", "East", "West", "West",
    "North", "North"
  ),
  PatronType = c(
    "Adult", "Child", "Adult", "Child",
    "Adult", "Child"
  ),
  Checkouts = c(45, 30, 60, 25, 40, 35)
)
```

1. Group the data by Library and calculate total checkouts for each one.

2. Group by PatronType and compute the average number of checkouts.

3. How many records are in each Library? Use n() in summarise().

4. Group by both Library and PatronType and calculate total checkouts.

5. Why might grouping by two variables be more informative than just one?

Data Set 2: Plant Growth Experiment

This dataset shows plant height measurements from different species in two test locations.

```
R Code
growth_data <- data.frame(
  Species = c(
    "Maple", "Maple", "Oak", "Oak",
    "Pine", "Pine"
  ),
  Location = c(
    "Greenhouse", "Field", "Greenhouse",
    "Field",
    "Greenhouse", "Field"
  ),
  Height_cm = c(150, 135, 160, 140, 180, 170)
)
```

6. Group by Species and find the average height.

7. Group by Location and compute total height.

8. Group by both Species and Location and find the average height.

9. Count how many entries exist per Location.

10. Which species-location combination had the tallest average height?

Data Set 3: Movie Ratings

This dataset contains ratings for movies from different genres, submitted by different user groups.

```
R Code
ratings_data <- data.frame(
  Genre = c("Comedy", "Comedy", "Drama", "Drama",
            "Action", "Action"),
  UserGroup = c("Teen", "Adult", "Teen", "Adult",
                "Teen", "Adult"),
  Rating = c(4.2, 3.8, 4.5, 4.0, 4.0, 3.5)
)
```

11. Group by Genre and find the average rating.

12. Group by UserGroup and calculate total ratings.

13. Group by both Genre and UserGroup to get average rating and count.

14. What does the count from question 13 represent in this context?

15. Why would an analyst want to compare ratings across both genre and user group?

Lab 21

Subset Data

Subsetting data means selecting certain parts of a dataset to focus your analysis or clean your data. You might want to select specific columns, filter rows that meet conditions, split data into training and testing groups, or remove rows with missing values.

Lesson Steps

Step 1: Subsetting Columns

Sometimes you only need a few columns from a larger dataset. Subsetting columns lets you extract only those variables that are important for your analysis. This can make your data easier to manage and reduce confusion caused by unnecessary information.

For example, if you have a dataset of students with their names, ages, grades, attendance, and state, but you just want a list of their names, you can subset to keep only the "Name" column.

R Code

```
# Create a dataset of students with multiple columns
students <- data.frame(
  Name = c("Alice", "Bob", "Carlos"),
  Age = c(15, 16, 15),
  Grade = c("A", "B", "A"),
  Attendance = c(95, 88, 92),
  State = c("NY", "CA", "TX")
)


# Keep only the Name column by selecting it with its name
students_subset <- students["Name"]


# View the result to confirm only the Name column is kept
students_subset
```

Output

```
##      Name
## 1  Alice
## 2    Bob
## 3 Carlos
```

Here, the output will show a data frame containing only the "Name" column with all the students' names. This is useful if you need a simple list or want to prepare a subset for further processing.

Step 2: Subsetting Rows

Instead of columns, you might want to filter the rows of a dataset to include only certain observations. For instance, you may want to focus on students who meet a specific condition, such as having attendance above 90%.

Subsetting rows allows you to create a smaller dataset containing only the records that satisfy your criteria. This helps you narrow your analysis to a targeted group.

R Code
```
# Using the same students dataset from Step 1


# Select only rows where Attendance is greater than 90
high_attendance <- students[students$Attendance > 90, ]


# View the filtered dataset
high_attendance
```

Output
```
##       Name Age Grade Attendance State
## 1  Alice   15    A         95    NY
## 3 Carlos   15    A         92    TX
```

In this example, only students with attendance greater than 90% will be kept. This is useful for identifying students who have strong attendance, which might be important for recognizing consistent participants or award eligibility.

267

Step 3: Subsetting for Train/Test Split

When building predictive models, it is a best practice to divide your data into a training set and a testing set. The training set is used to build the model, and the testing set is used to evaluate how well the model performs on new, unseen data.

Randomly selecting which data goes into training and testing sets helps avoid bias. This step is essential in machine learning workflows to get realistic estimates of model accuracy.

R Code

```
# Create a small dataset of student test scores

students <- data.frame(
  Name = c("Alice", "Bob", "Carlos", "Diana", "Ethan"),
  Math_Score = c(90, 85, 78, 92, 88),
  Reading_Score = c(87, 80, 75, 95, 90)
)


# Set a random seed to make the sampling reproducible
set.seed(42)


# Find how many rows are in the dataset
n <- nrow(students)


# Randomly sample 80% of the rows for the training set
train_indices <- sample(1:n, size = 0.8 * n)


# Use the sampled indices to create the training set
train_data <- students[train_indices, ]


# Use the remaining rows for the testing set
test_data <- students[-train_indices, ]


# View the training data
train_data
```

Output

```
##        Name Math_Score Reading_Score
## 1  Alice           90            87
## 5  Ethan           88            90
## 4  Diana           92            95
## 3 Carlos           78            75
```

R Code

```r
# View the testing data
test_data
```

Output

```
##     Name Math_Score Reading_Score
## 2  Bob           85            80
```

This process splits the data randomly. About 80% of the data becomes training data, and 20% becomes testing data. Setting the seed ensures you get the same split every time you run the code.

Step 4: Subsetting to Handle Missing Data

Real-world datasets often contain missing values. These missing values can cause errors or bias in your analysis if not handled properly. One simple way to deal with missing data is to remove any rows that contain missing values.

Removing incomplete rows ensures that your analysis is based on complete data records, which can improve reliability, especially in smaller datasets.

R Code
```
# Create a dataset with some missing values
survey <- data.frame(
  Name = c("Alice", "Bob", "Carlos"),
  Age = c(15, NA, 16),
  Grade = c("A", "B", NA),
  Feedback = c("Good", NA, "Excellent")
)

# Remove any rows that contain missing values in any column
survey_clean <- na.omit(survey)

# View the cleaned dataset without missing values
survey_clean
```

Output
```
##     Name Age Grade Feedback
## 1 Alice  15     A     Good
```

After running this code, the dataset will only contain rows where every column has data. This cleaning step is quick and effective when missing values are relatively few.

Wrap-Up

Subsetting data is a powerful way to focus your analysis and prepare your data for modeling or reporting. Selecting columns narrows variables, filtering rows targets specific observations, splitting data supports model training and testing, and removing missing data ensures complete cases.

Exercises

Subset Data

Subsetting lets you isolate parts of your data based on your needs—just certain columns, specific rows, a random train/test split, or complete rows without missing values. These exercises will help you practice each type of subsetting.

Data Set 1: Employee Records

This dataset tracks information for five employees.

```
R Code
employees <- data.frame(
  Name = c("Janet", "Marcus", "Leo", "Priya", "Tom"),
  Department = c("HR", "IT", "IT", "Finance", "HR"),
  Salary = c(55000, 72000, 69000, 80000, 56000),
  City = c("NY", "LA", "NY", "SF", "LA")
)
```

1. Subset only the Name and Department columns.

2. Subset the rows for employees in the "HR" department.

3. Subset the rows where Salary is greater than 60000.

Data Set 2: Course Completion

This dataset shows students' completion status for two courses.

R Code
```
course_data <- data.frame(
  Student = c("Ana", "Brian", "Clara", "David", "Ella"),
  Math_Complete = c(TRUE, TRUE, FALSE, TRUE, FALSE),
  Science_Complete = c(TRUE, FALSE, TRUE, TRUE, TRUE)
)
```

4. Subset to show only students who completed both courses.

5. Subset to show only the Student and Math_Complete columns.

6. Subset to show rows where Science_Complete is FALSE.

Data Set 3: Customer Feedback

This dataset includes some missing responses.

R Code
```
feedback <- data.frame(
  Customer = c("C1", "C2", "C3", "C4"),
  Rating = c(5, NA, 4, NA),
  Comment = c("Great", "Okay", NA, "Good")
)
```

7. Subset the rows that have no missing values.

8. How many rows were removed by na.omit()?

9. What might be a reason to keep rather than delete rows with missing values?

Data Set 4: Product Prices (Train/Test Split)

This dataset shows prices for five products.

```
R Code
products <- data.frame(
  Product = c("A", "B", "C", "D", "E"),
  Price = c(12.5, 9.8, 15.0, 8.7, 11.0),
  Category = c("Snacks", "Drinks", "Snacks",
               "Drinks", "Snacks")
)
```

10. Use set.seed(1) and randomly split 80% of the data into a training set.

11. What rows are in the training set?

12. What rows are in the testing set?

Lab 22

Restructuring Data

Introduction

Restructuring data means changing the shape or layout of your dataset to better suit your analysis. Depending on the problem, you might need to switch between wide and long formats, transpose your data, or combine and separate datasets vertically. This lab shows you common ways to reshape your data in R.

Lesson Steps

Step 1: Melting Data — Wide to Long Format

Wide vs. Long Format

Data can be organized in wide format, where repeated measures are stored in multiple columns, or long format, where those repeated values are stacked into rows. Many R functions and packages work best with long format data because it makes grouping and summarizing easier.

Melting means turning multiple columns of related data into two columns: one for the variable name (like "Subject") and one for the value (like "Score").

This is useful for analyses that need tidy long-format data.

```
R Code
# Load tidyr package for reshaping functions
library(tidyr)

# Create a sample dataset in wide format:
# student scores by subject
scores <- data.frame(
  Name = c("Alex", "Brian", "Cathy"),
  Math = c(85, 78, 92),
  Science = c(90, 88, 95)
)

# Convert from wide to long format using pivot_longer
long_scores <- pivot_longer(
  scores,
  # Columns to melt into long format
  cols = c(Math, Science),

  # Name of the new column that will hold the old column names
  names_to = "Subject",

  # Name of the new column that will hold the values
  values_to = "Score"
)

# View the original wide data
print(scores)
```

Output

```
##      Name Math Science
## 1  Alex    85      90
## 2 Brian    78      88
## 3 Cathy    92      95
```

R Code

```
# View the transformed long data
print(long_scores)
```

Output

```
## # A tibble: 6 x 3
##    Name  Subject Score
##    <chr> <chr>   <dbl>
## 1 Alex   Math       85
## 2 Alex   Science    90
## 3 Brian  Math       78
## 4 Brian  Science    88
## 5 Cathy  Math       92
## 6 Cathy  Science    95
```

Here, the Math and Science columns are "melted" into two columns: Subject (with values "Math" or "Science") and Score (with the respective scores). This long format is tidier for many R analyses.

Step 2: Pivoting Data — Long to Wide Format

Pivoting is the reverse of melting. It turns long format data back into wide format by spreading values across multiple columns. This is often useful for reporting or exporting data in a readable format.

```
R Code
# Load tidyr package
library(tidyr)


# Example of long-format data with student scores
long_scores <- data.frame(
  Name = c(
    "Alex", "Alex", "Brian", "Brian", "Cathy",
    "Cathy"
  ),
  Subject = c(
    "Math", "Science", "Math", "Science",
    "Math", "Science"
  ),
  Score = c(85, 90, 78, 88, 92, 95)
)


# Convert from long to wide format using pivot_wider
wide_scores <- pivot_wider(
  long_scores,
  # Column whose values will become new columns
  names_from = Subject,
  # Column with values to fill new columns
  values_from = Score
)
```

```
# View the original long data
print(long_scores)
```

Output

```
##      Name Subject Score
## 1  Alex    Math    85
## 2  Alex Science    90
## 3 Brian    Math    78
## 4 Brian Science    88
## 5 Cathy    Math    92
## 6 Cathy Science    95
```

R Code

```
# View the new wide data
print(wide_scores)
```

Output

```
## # A tibble: 3 x 3
##    Name   Math Science
##    <chr> <dbl>   <dbl>
## 1 Alex     85      90
## 2 Brian    78      88
## 3 Cathy    92      95
```

Each unique value in the Subject column (like "Math" and "Science") becomes its own column again, with scores filled in.

Step 3: Transposing — Flipping Rows and Columns

Transposing flips the dataset so that rows become columns and columns become rows. This can be useful for quick data views or special formats.

R Code
```r
# Create a sample wide-format data frame
scores <- data.frame(
  Name = c("Alex", "Brian", "Cathy"),
  Math = c(85, 78, 92),
  Science = c(90, 88, 95)
)

# Transpose the dataset using base R's t() function
transposed <- t(scores)

# View original data before transpose
print(scores)
```

Output
```
##      Name Math Science
## 1   Alex   85      90
## 2 Brian   78      88
## 3 Cathy   92      95
```

R Code
```r
# View data after transpose (note this becomes a matrix)
print(transposed)
```

Output

```
##            [,1]    [,2]    [,3]
## Name     "Alex"  "Brian" "Cathy"
## Math     "85"    "78"    "92"
## Science  "90"    "88"    "95"
```

After transposing, what were columns are now rows, and what were rows are now columns. The row names become column names and vice versa.

Step 4: Stacking — Combining Datasets Vertically

Stacking means putting together datasets with the same columns by adding rows. This is useful when you have data from multiple time periods or batches and want to analyze it as one dataset.

R Code
```
# Create sample sales data for January
jan <- data.frame(
  Product = c("A", "B"),
  Sales = c(100, 150)
)


# Create sample sales data for February
feb <- data.frame(
  Product = c("A", "B"),
  Sales = c(120, 130)
)


# Stack the two months vertically using rbind()
stacked <- rbind(jan, feb)


# View the combined dataset
print(stacked)
```

Output
```
##    Product Sales
## 1        A    100
## 2        B    150
## 3        A    120
## 4        B    130
```

The stacked dataset now contains all rows from January and February, one after the other.

Step 5: Unstacking — Splitting Data into Groups

Unstacking splits a dataset into groups based on a variable, creating separate subsets. This is useful for separate analyses or reporting by group.

```
R Code
# Split the stacked sales data by Product
split_data <- split(stacked, stacked$Product)


# View the list of split datasets
print(split_data)
```

```
Output
## $A
##    Product Sales
## 1       A    100
## 3       A    120
##
## $B
##    Product Sales
## 2       B    150
## 4       B    130
```

The result is a list where each element is a data frame containing sales for one product.

Wrap-Up

This lab introduced several key data reshaping techniques in R. Melting is the process of converting wide-format data into long format by turning repeated measures into rows. Pivoting does the reverse, transforming long-format data back into wide format by spreading values across columns. Transposing switches rows and columns, which can be useful for reorienting a dataset. Stacking combines multiple datasets vertically by adding rows, while unstacking separates a dataset into subgroups based on a chosen variable. Together, these tools allow you to reshape your data into the form best suited for analysis, visualization, or reporting tasks.

Exercises

Restructuring Data

These exercises walk you through the five major data restructuring techniques in R: melting, pivoting, transposing, stacking, and unstacking.

Data Set 1: Grades by Subject (Wide to Long)

```
R Code
grades <- data.frame(
  Student = c("Amy", "Ben", "Cara"),
  History = c(88, 76, 91),
  English = c(93, 85, 87)
)
```

1. Use pivot_longer() to convert this dataset into long format.

2. What are the names of the new columns?

3. How many rows are in the resulting long-format dataset?

Data Set 2: Grades Long Format (Long to Wide)

```
R Code
long_grades <- data.frame(
  Student = c(
    "Amy", "Amy", "Ben", "Ben", "Cara",
    "Cara"
  ),
  Subject = c(
    "History", "English", "History",
    "English", "History", "English"
  ),
  Score = c(88, 93, 76, 85, 91, 87)
)
```

4. Use pivot_wider() to convert this long-format data into wide format.

5. Which function argument tells R which column becomes the new column names?

6. What does the final wide-format table look like?

Data Set 3: Store Sales (Transpose)

```
R Code
sales <- data.frame(
  Month = c("Jan", "Feb", "Mar"),
  Online = c(200, 250, 220),
  InStore = c(180, 190, 210)
)
```

7. Use t() to transpose this dataset.

8. What type of object is the result of t()?

9. In your output, what becomes the new row names?

Data Set 4: Website Traffic (Stacking)

```
R Code
week1 <- data.frame(
  Day = c("Mon", "Tue"),
  Visits = c(300, 280)
)


week2 <- data.frame(
  Day = c("Wed", "Thu"),
  Visits = c(310, 290)
)
```

10. Stack week1 and week2 using rbind().

11. How many rows are in the stacked result?

12. Why would you stack data from multiple weeks?

Data Set 5: Feedback by Category (Unstacking)

```
R Code
feedback <- data.frame(
  Type = c("Positive", "Positive", "Negative",
           "Negative"),
  Score = c(5, 4, 2, 1)
)
```

13. Use split() to unstack this data by the Type column.

14. What are the names of the list elements?

15. How many rows are in each group?

Lab 23

Merging and Joining Data

Introduction

In real-world data analysis, we often need to combine information from multiple sources—especially when each dataset holds different pieces of related information. This lab focuses on merging and joining datasets, which allow you to link tables based on shared keys or identifiers. Unlike stacking or unstacking, which rearrange or append data, merging creates connections between datasets horizontally, adding columns from one table to another. This process is essential when preparing data for analysis, as it lets you bring together complementary variables from different sources into one complete dataset.

Lesson Steps

Step 1: Understand Merging (Joining)

Merging, also called joining, is the process of combining two datasets side-by-side by adding columns from one dataset to another. This is done based on a shared key—a unique identifier like a customer ID or student number that exists in both datasets. In R, you can perform merging using the base

merge() function or the join functions from the dplyr package, such as in-
ner_join(), left_join(), and others.

Step 2: Create Sample Data for Joining

Before performing joins, let's create two example datasets—a customer table and an orders table—that share a common key (ID) to demonstrate how
merging works in practice.

```
R Code
library(dplyr)

# Customers table
df1 <- data.frame(
   ID = c(1, 2, 3, 4),
   Name = c("Alex", "Sam", "Casey", "Riley")
)

# Orders table
df2 <- data.frame(
   ID = c(2, 3, 4, 5),
   Order = c("Book", "Pen", "Notebook", "Bag")
)

print(df1)
```

Output
```
##   ID  Name
## 1  1  Alex
## 2  2   Sam
## 3  3 Casey
## 4  4 Riley
```

R Code
```
print(df2)
```

Output
```
##   ID     Order
## 1  2      Book
## 2  3       Pen
## 3  4  Notebook
## 4  5       Bag
```

Step 3: Perform Different Types of Joins

3.1 Inner Join

An inner join keeps only the rows where keys match in both tables.

R Code
```
inner_join(df1, df2, by = "ID")
```

Output
```
##   ID  Name    Order
## 1  2   Sam     Book
## 2  3 Casey      Pen
## 3  4 Riley Notebook
```

Use this when you want to analyze only records present in **both** datasets. **Example:** Find customers who have placed orders. This excludes customers without orders and orders without matching customers.

3.2 Left Join

A left join keeps all rows from the left table (df1) and adds matching columns from the right (df2). Non-matching rows from the right table become NA.

R Code
```
left_join(df1, df2, by = "ID")
```

Output
```
##   ID  Name    Order
## 1  1  Alex     <NA>
## 2  2   Sam     Book
## 3  3 Casey      Pen
## 4  4 Riley Notebook
```

Use this when your main focus is the left dataset and you want to include additional info if available. **Example:** Get a full list of customers with their orders if any. Customers without orders show NA in order columns.

3.3 Right Join

A right join keeps all rows from the right table (df2) and adds matching columns from the left (df1). Non-matching rows from the left table become NA.

R Code
```
right_join(df1, df2, by = "ID")
```

Output
```
##    ID  Name     Order
## 1  2   Sam       Book
## 2  3 Casey        Pen
## 3  4 Riley  Notebook
## 4  5  <NA>        Bag
```

Use this when the right dataset is your focus and you want to attach info from the left. **Example:** List all orders with customer info when available, even if some orders have unknown customers.

3.4 Full Join

A full join keeps all rows from both tables, matching where possible and filling unmatched rows with NA.

R Code
```
full_join(df1, df2, by = "ID")
```

293

Output

```
##    ID  Name    Order
## 1  1   Alex    <NA>
## 2  2   Sam     Book
## 3  3 Casey     Pen
## 4  4 Riley Notebook
## 5  5  <NA>     Bag
```

Use this when you want to combine all records from both datasets, preserving unmatched rows from both sides. An example of when you may want to do this is to create a complete table of all customers and all orders, including customers without orders and orders without customers.

Step 4: Common Issues and Precautions When Merging

When merging datasets, it's important to be aware of some common issues that can affect your results and how to handle them.

First, missing keys in one dataset can cause rows to be dropped or have missing values (NA) in the merged output. For example, if a key exists in one table but not the other, an inner join will exclude that row entirely, while outer joins will keep it but fill unmatched columns with NA.

Second, duplicate keys in either dataset can lead to unexpected row multiplication. This happens because the merge pairs every matching key from one dataset with every matching key in the other, which can increase the number of rows and cause confusion.

Third, merging very large datasets may slow down your processing or even cause your system to crash if memory is insufficient. Always be cautious with large joins.

Best practices to avoid problems when merging data include checking the number of rows before and after the join to see if any rows were lost or added unexpectedly. You should also remove duplicate keys using the dis-tinct() function to ensure that each key is unique, which helps prevent acci-dental row multiplication. To identify records that exist in one dataset but not the other, use anti_join()—this helps you spot mismatches and clean up your data before performing the final merge.

Here is how you can use `anti_join()` to find unmatched keys:

```
R Code
# Find IDs in df1 that are not in df2
anti_join(df1, df2, by = "ID")
```

```
Output
##    ID Name
## 1   1 Alex
```

```
R Code
# Find IDs in df2 that are not in df1
anti_join(df2, df1, by = "ID")
```

```
Output
##    ID Order
## 1   5   Bag
```

Running these commands will show you which rows in one dataset do not have a corresponding match in the other. This helps you decide whether to exclude those records, fill missing data, or correct mismatches before merging.

Wrap-Up

Merging, or joining, lets you combine related datasets side-by-side based on shared keys, allowing you to enrich your data with additional information. You practiced different types of joins—inner, left, right, and full—and understood when to use each depending on whether you want only matching records or to keep all data with possible missing matches. Finally, you explored common challenges such as missing or duplicate keys and large dataset performance, along with best practices like checking for unmatched rows and duplicates before merging.

Exercises

**Merging and Joining Data*

Data Set 1: Merging with Joins

```
R Code
customers <- data.frame(
  ID = c(101, 102, 103, 104),
  Name = c("Ann", "Ben", "Clara", "Dan")
)

orders <- data.frame(
  ID = c(102, 103, 105),
  Product = c("Book", "Pen", "Laptop")
)
```

1. Perform inner_join(customers, orders, by = "ID"). What does it show?

2. Perform left_join(customers, orders, by = "ID"). What additional info is included?

3. Perform right_join(customers, orders, by = "ID"). What extra rows appear?

4. Perform full_join(customers, orders, by = "ID"). How many NAs and why?

5. Which join shows all customers even if they have no orders?

6. Which join shows all orders even if customer info is missing?

7. Use anti_join(customers, orders, by = "ID") to find customers without orders.

8. Use anti_join(orders, customers, by = "ID") to find orders without matching customers.

9. Why is anti_join() useful when merging?

Data Set 2: Duplicate Keys

```
R Code
contacts <- data.frame(
  ID = c(201, 202, 202, 203),
  Name = c("Eli", "Fran", "Fran", "Gina")
)


appointments <- data.frame(
  ID = c(202, 203, 204),
  Time = c("10AM", "11AM", "12PM")
)
```

10. Perform inner_join(contacts, appointments, by = "ID"). Why are there more rows than original datasets? Explain row multiplication.

Lab 24

SQL for Data Restructuring (in R)

Introduction

SQL (Structured Query Language) is one of the most powerful and widely used tools for managing and restructuring data. It allows you to filter, join, aggregate, and transform data quickly and efficiently. Even when working in R, knowing how to use SQL queries can greatly simplify complex data tasks, especially when dealing with large datasets or databases.

In this lesson, you will learn how to run SQL queries directly inside R to restructure your data. This approach combines the flexibility of R with the power of SQL, making it easier to perform advanced data manipulations without switching environments.

Lesson Steps

Step 1: Setup — Using SQL inside R

To use SQL queries directly on data frames in R, install and load the sqldf package, which lets you run SQL commands on R data frames.

R Code
```
# Install if not already installed

options(repos = c(CRAN = "https://cran.r-project.org"))
install.packages("sqldf")
library(sqldf)
```

Step 2: Create Sample Data

Start with two example data frames: students and major.

R Code
```
students <- data.frame(
  ID = 1:5,
  Name = c("Kim", "Lee", "Pat", "Alex", "Sam"),
  Year = c(2024, 2023, 2024, 2023, 2025),
  Score = c(88, 92, 75, 85, 90)
)

majors <- data.frame(
  ID = c(1, 3, 4, 6),
  Major = c("Math", "Biology", "History", "Physics")
)

students
```

Output

```
##    ID Name Year Score
## 1  1   Kim 2024    88
## 2  2   Lee 2023    92
## 3  3   Pat 2024    75
## 4  4  Alex 2023    85
## 5  5   Sam 2025    90
```

R Code

```
majors
```

Output

```
##    ID    Major
## 1  1     Math
## 2  3   Biology
## 3  4   History
## 4  6   Physics
```

Step 3: SELECT — Picking and Rearranging Columns

The SELECT statement in SQL lets you specify exactly which columns you want to retrieve from a table. This is useful when you don't need all the data, only certain fields, or when you want to change the order of columns in your output.

To select only the Name and Score columns from the students table using SQL syntax inside R:

R Code

```
selected_data <- sqldf("SELECT Name, Score FROM students")
print(selected_data)
```

Output

```
##    Name Score
## 1  Kim    88
## 2  Lee    92
## 3  Pat    75
## 4 Alex    85
## 5  Sam    90
```

This query returns a new data frame with just the Name and Score columns.

You can also rearrange columns by changing their order in the SELECT clause:

R Code

```
rearranged_data <- sqldf("SELECT Score, Name FROM students")
print(rearranged_data)
```

Output

```
##    Score Name
## 1    88  Kim
## 2    92  Lee
## 3    75  Pat
## 4    85 Alex
## 5    90  Sam
```

If you want all columns, use SELECT *:

```
R Code
all_columns <- sqldf("SELECT * FROM students")
print(all_columns)
```

```
Output
##    ID Name Year Score
## 1  1  Kim 2024    88
## 2  2  Lee 2023    92
## 3  3  Pat 2024    75
## 4  4 Alex 2023    85
## 5  5  Sam 2025    90
```

Step 4: CREATE TABLE AS SELECT

Create a new table based on filtered data from an existing table. For example, select students who scored above 90.

```
R Code
top_students <-
  sqldf("SELECT Name, Score FROM students WHERE Score > 90")
top_students
```

```
Output
##   Name Score
## 1  Lee    92
```

This creates a new data frame top_students with only high-scoring students.

Step 5: WHERE — Filtering Rows

The WHERE clause in SQL is used to filter rows based on specified conditions. It works like a filter that lets you select only the rows meeting certain criteria. For example, find students from the year 2024.

R Code
```
sqldf("SELECT * FROM students WHERE Year = 2024")
```

Output
```
##    ID Name Year Score
## 1  1  Kim 2024    88
## 2  3  Pat 2024    75
```

This returns all columns for students in 2024.

Step 6: GROUP BY — Summarizing Data by Groups

Grouping means combining rows that share the same value in a particular column. After grouping, you can calculate summary statistics for each group, such as counting how many rows are in the group, finding the average value in a numeric column, or summing values within the group. In SQL, you use the GROUP BY clause to group rows based on a column's values. Then, you apply aggregate functions like COUNT() to count the number of rows in each group, AVG() to calculate the average value of a column within each group, and SUM() to add up the values of a column for each group.

For example, count how many students are in each academic year.

R Code

```
sqldf("SELECT Year,
       COUNT(*) AS NumStudents FROM students GROUP BY Year")
```

Output

```
##    Year NumStudents
## 1 2023           2
## 2 2024           2
## 3 2025           1
```

This returns the number of students per year.

Step 7: HAVING — Filtering Groups After Aggregation

The HAVING clause is used to filter the results after rows have been grouped with GROUP BY. While WHERE filters individual rows before grouping, HAVING filters groups based on aggregate conditions. For example, if you group students by their academic year and count how many students are in each group, HAVING lets you keep only those groups where the count meets a condition, like having more than 2 students. This means you can ask the database to show only the years that have enough students, filtering out groups that are too small. The HAVING clause works together with aggregate functions like COUNT(), SUM(), or AVG() to filter groups based on those calculations.

R Code
```
library(sqldf)

query <- paste(
  "SELECT Year,",
  "COUNT(*) AS NumStudents",
  "FROM students",
  "GROUP BY Year",
  "HAVING NumStudents > 2",
  sep = " "
)

sqldf(query)
```

Output
```
## [1] Year         NumStudents
## <0 rows> (or 0-length row.names)
```

This returns only years where the number of students exceeds 2.

Step 8: ORDER BY — Sorting Query Results

Sort the query output by one or more columns using the ORDER BY clause. You can sort in ascending order (ASC), which is the default and arranges values from lowest to highest, or in descending order (DESC), which arranges values from highest to lowest.

For example, to order students by their score in descending order (highest to lowest):

R Code
```
sqldf("SELECT Name, Score FROM students ORDER BY Score DESC")
```

Output
```
##    Name Score
## 1  Lee    92
## 2  Sam    90
## 3  Kim    88
## 4 Alex    85
## 5  Pat    75
```

To order students by their score in ascending order (lowest to highest):

R Code
```
sqldf("SELECT Name, Score FROM students ORDER BY Score ASC")
```

Output
```
##    Name Score
## 1  Pat    75
## 2 Alex    85
## 3  Kim    88
## 4  Sam    90
## 5  Lee    92
```

These commands help you view the data sorted in the way that best suits your analysis.

Step 9: JOIN — Combining Tables Horizontally

Suppose you have these two tables:

```
R Code
library(sqldf)

students <- data.frame(
  ID = c(1, 2, 3, 4),
  Name = c("Alice", "Bob", "Carlos", "Dana"),
  Year = c(2023, 2024, 2023, 2025),
  Score = c(85, 90, 88, 92)
)

majors <- data.frame(
  ID = c(2, 3, 5),
  Major = c("Math", "Physics", "Biology")
)

students
```

```
Output
##    ID    Name Year Score
## 1  1   Alice 2023    85
## 2  2     Bob 2024    90
## 3  3  Carlos 2023    88
## 4  4    Dana 2025    92
```

```
R Code
majors
```

Output
```
##   ID   Major
## 1  2    Math
## 2  3 Physics
## 3  5 Biology
```

Inner Join: Keep only rows with matching IDs in both tables

Note that in joins in SQL, aliasing is used to give each table a short nickname. The table students is given the alias s, and the table majors is given the alias m. This means that instead of writing the full table name each time, the query can use s to refer to students and m to refer to majors. For example, s.ID refers to the ID column in the students table, and m.Major refers to the Major column in the majors table. Aliasing helps make the query easier to read and type, especially when dealing with long table names or when joining multiple tables. It also helps avoid confusion if both tables have columns with the same name.

R Code
```
sqldf("
  SELECT s.ID, s.Name, s.Year, s.Score, m.Major
  FROM students s
  JOIN majors m ON s.ID = m.ID
")
```

Output
```
##   ID   Name Year Score   Major
## 1  2    Bob 2024    90    Math
## 2  3 Carlos 2023    88 Physics
```

Only students who have a matching major appear. Students without majors and majors without students are excluded.

Left Join: Keep all rows from students plus matching majors if they exist

R Code
```
sqldf("
  SELECT s.ID, s.Name, s.Year, s.Score, m.Major
  FROM students s
  LEFT JOIN majors m ON s.ID = m.ID
")
```

Output
```
##   ID   Name Year Score   Major
## 1  1  Alice 2023    85    <NA>
## 2  2    Bob 2024    90    Math
## 3  3 Carlos 2023    88 Physics
## 4  4   Dana 2025    92    <NA>
```

All students are included. Majors are added if they match. Students without a major show NULL in the Major column. Majors without students are excluded.

Right Join: Keep all rows from majors plus matching students if they exist

```
R Code
sqldf("
  SELECT s.ID, s.Name, s.Year, s.Score, m.Major
  FROM students s
  RIGHT JOIN majors m ON s.ID = m.ID
")
```

```
Output
##    ID   Name Year Score    Major
## 1  2    Bob 2024    90     Math
## 2  3 Carlos 2023    88 Physics
## 3 NA   <NA>   NA    NA Biology
```

All majors are included. Students are added if they match. Majors without students show NULL for student info. Students without majors are excluded.

Full Join: Keep all rows from both tables, matching where possible

SQLite (used by sqldf) does not support FULL JOIN directly, but you can simulate it by combining left and right joins with UNION:

R Code

```
sqldf("
  SELECT s.ID, s.Name, s.Year, s.Score, m.Major
  FROM students s
  LEFT JOIN majors m ON s.ID = m.ID

  UNION

  SELECT m.ID, NULL AS Name, NULL AS Year,
  NULL AS Score, m.Major
  FROM majors m
  LEFT JOIN students s ON s.ID = m.ID
  WHERE s.ID IS NULL
")
```

Output

```
##    ID   Name Year Score   Major
## 1  1  Alice 2023    85    <NA>
## 2  2    Bob 2024    90    Math
## 3  3  Carlos 2023   88 Physics
## 4  4   Dana 2025    92    <NA>
## 5  5   <NA>   NA    NA Biology
```

This returns all students and all majors. Matching rows are combined. Non-matching students or majors appear with missing values (NULL) on the opposite side.

Wrap-Up

In this lab, you learned how to use SQL queries within R to restructure and analyze data efficiently. You practiced selecting and rearranging columns, filtering rows with WHERE, grouping data with GROUP BY and filtering groups with HAVING. You also sorted results using ORDER BY in both ascending and descending order.

Importantly, you explored different ways to combine tables using JOINs: inner join for matching rows, left join for all rows in the first table, right join for all rows in the second table, and how to simulate full joins in SQLite by combining left and right joins with a union.

Using SQL inside R with the sqldf package combines the flexibility of R with the power of SQL, enabling you to perform complex data restructuring tasks without switching environments. Mastering these SQL commands will greatly enhance your data manipulation skills and help you work more efficiently with data frames and databases.

Keep practicing these queries on your own data to become comfortable with the syntax and logic of SQL in R.

Exercises

SQL for Data Restructuring

Data

```
R Code
library(sqldf)
students <- data.frame(
  ID = 1:8,
  Name = c(
    "Dana", "Ravi", "Chris", "Jordan",
    "Sky", "Morgan", "Taylor", "Casey"
  ),
  Year = c(
    2025, 2023, 2024, 2025, 2023,
    2024, 2024, 2023
  ),
  Score = c(78, 89, 91, 83, 76, 95, 88, 80)
)

majors <- data.frame(
  ID = c(2, 3, 5, 7, 8),
  Major = c(
    "Chemistry", "Philosophy", "English",
    "Economics", "Art"
  )
)
```

1. Select only the Name and Score columns from students.

2. Select Score and Name columns in reverse order.

3. Select all columns from students.

4. Create a new table of students who scored above 85.

5. Retrieve all columns for students in the year 2023.

6. Count how many students are in each year (group by `Year`).

7. Show only the years where the number of students is greater than 1.

8. Order the students by their Score descending.

9. Order the students by their Score ascending.

10. Perform an inner join between students and majors on ID — show all student info plus their major.

11. Perform a left join of students and majors — include all students and add majors if they exist.

12. Perform a right join of students and majors — include all majors and add students if they exist.

13. Simulate a full join of students and majors — include all students and all majors, matching when possible.

14. Explain the difference between WHERE and HAVING clauses in SQL.

15. Why might you prefer to use SQL in R when restructuring large datasets?

www.ingramcontent.com/pod-product-compliance
Lightning Source LLC
Chambersburg PA
CBHW051714210326
41597CB00032B/5475